MW01671139

Linking Language and the Environment

Greening the ESL Classroom

GEORGE M. JACOBS

PRAMARANEE M. KUMARASAMY

PAYOMRAT NOPPARAT

SUSAN AMY

Pippin Publishing

Suite 232, 85 Ellesmere Road
Toronto, Ontario
M1R 4B9

Designed by John Zehethofer
Edited by Helen Mason
Typeset by Jay Tee Graphics Ltd.
Printed and bound in Canada by Friesens

Canadian Cataloguing in Publication Data

Main entry under title:

Linking language and the environment

(The Pippin teacher's library; 32)
Includes bibliographical references.
ISBN 0-88751-092-2

1. English language — Study and teaching as a second language. 2. Environmental education. 3. Environmental protection — Problem, exercises, etc. I. Jacobs, George M. II. Title. III. Series.

PE1128.A2L564 1998 428'.0071'5 C98-930575-9

ISBN 0-88751-092-2

10 9 8 7 6 5 4 3 2 1

CONTENTS

ACKNOWLEDGMENTS

We gratefully acknowledge Lim Poh Bee, who was of great assistance to us in the early stages of our writing, and our students, who have helped erode our misconceptions about second language teaching and whose interest in protecting the environment inspired us to create this book. We also acknowledge the talent and perseverance of those who work full-time in environmental organizations. Last, but not least, we owe a debt of gratitude to Helen Mason for her skillful and sympathetic editing.

As our own commitment to the environment, we will be donating all our royalties from this book to environmental organizations in the countries where we live.

INTRODUCTION

This is a book about how we can integrate environmental education into language instruction. We in language education know about the mounting levels of environmental destruction going on all around us. Whether the problem is hundreds of miles away or as close as the air we are breathing, many of us feel frustrated by our seeming inability to do our part in protecting the environment. Fortunately, in our professional capacities, we can join with students and colleagues to promote environmental protection at the same time that we promote language learning. This book offers some ideas on how to achieve this goal. No doubt, you, your students and colleagues already have many more ideas. It is not necessary to have a degree in biology to develop and use environmental education activities. Such activities can be integrated into language instruction by anyone interested in protecting the environment. Even better, they can complement the mandatory curriculum.

Why integrate environmental education into language instruction? We humans are destroying the environment of our beautiful planet Earth at an amazing speed. Most of this environmental devastation is caused by people who are educated and understand the blight they are producing. It is ironic that many of those who live sustainably on the Earth are traditional peoples who have no formal education and do not know how to read or write. This shows that education is no guarantee of environmental awareness or care. Perhaps the key is not whether one has lots of scientific knowledge or can read and write several languages with perfect grammar, but whether or not the content of that education is put to good use. This book is intended to provide students with appropriate content and show them how to use it.

The book has two main parts. "Part I: Environmental Education and Language Instruction" provides background information. "Part II: Environmental Lessons" is a collection of lessons teachers can use to coach students in using language to learn about and act on behalf of the environment.

"Part I: Environmental Education and Language Instruction" is divided into four sections:

— The opening section gives a sketch of what environmental education is.
— The second section discusses how environmental education fits well with current trends in language education.
— The third gives some answers to frequently asked questions about integrating environmental education and language instruction.
— The fourth provides an overview of the components of the lessons which make up the rest of the book.
— Since many of the activities involve group interaction, the final section also outlines some techniques for facilitating group work.

"Part II: Environmental Lessons" provides a set of lessons with environmental content for students of English. These lessons can easily be adapted for learners of other languages. They are intended for 12- to 19-year-old students of at least high beginner proficiency level; however, they can also be used with adult language learners. By "high beginner," we mean students who can hold a conversation, write a short composition and comprehend a simple reading or listening passage. Such students have a vocabulary of at least 800 words. With this level of vocabulary, they will need some support to complete the activities presented here. Necessary support can include pre-teaching relevant vocabulary using pictures, gestures and discussion.

We hope that you will find this book easy to read and enjoyable to use. It provides ideas that will help novice and experienced teachers integrate environmental learning into the language classroom. These ideas and the accompanying methodology are very much in line with current thinking on language curriculum and modern teaching methods. We think that the following poem produced by the United Nations Environmental Sabbath Program best communicates our main goal in developing both the activities and the book:

A Prayer for Healing

We join with the earth and with each other.

To bring new life to the land
To restore the waters
To refresh the air

We join with the earth and with each other.

To renew the forests
To care for the plants
To protect the creatures

We join with the earth and with each other.

To celebrate the seas
To rejoice in the sunlight
To sing the song of the stars

We join with the earth and with each other.

To recreate the human community
To promote justice and peace
To remember our children

We join with the earth and with each other.

We join together as many and diverse expressions
of one loving mystery: for the healing of the earth and the renewal of all life.

ENVIRONMENTAL EDUCATION AND LANGUAGE INSTRUCTION

If you are thinking a year ahead, sow seed;
If you are thinking ten years ahead, plant a tree;
If you are thinking 100 years ahead, educate the people.

Kuan Tzu, 400 BC

In order to teach language through environmental education, we must first understand what environmental education is. Environmental education emerged in the 1970s in recognition of the rapidly escalating deterioration of the environment. In 1975, the United Nations organized an International Environmental Education Workshop in Belgrade, Yugoslavia. The key result of this workshop was the Belgrade Charter, which recognized the pressing necessity of environmental education and elaborated the following six objectives for the field:

— *Awareness:* Involves acquiring an awareness of and sensitivity to the total environment and its allied problems. For example, people need to be aware of deteriorating air quality and the dangers it poses.
— *Knowledge:* Involves acquiring basic understanding of the total environment, its associated problems and humanity's critically responsible presence and role. For example, people need to be aware of the causes of air pollution and recognize possible solutions to the problem.
— *Attitude:* Involves acquiring social values, strong feelings of concern for the environment and the motivation for actively participating in environmental protection and improvement. For example, people need to care about the destruc-

tion which air pollution causes and want to do something about it.

- *Skills:* Involves acquiring the skills for solving environmental problems. These include scientific and technological skills, as well as language skills. For example, language ability helps people write materials that inform others about the risks caused by air pollution. Similarly, oral language skills are important in convincing people to take action to decrease air pollution.
- *Evaluative Ability:* Involves developing the skills to evaluate environmental measures and educational programs in terms of ecological, political, economic, social, esthetic and educational factors. While everyone agrees that we must do something to protect the environment, there is disagreement about how to do it. For example, should we restrict car ownership in an effort to lessen air pollution or increase efforts to decrease exhaust emissions?
- *Participation:* Involves developing a sense of responsibility and urgency regarding environmental problems. This would ensure appropriate action to solve those problems. Participation is vital because all the other objectives come to nothing if people do not translate their awareness, knowledge, attitudes, skills and evaluative ability into action.

In our view, too many environmental education materials stop at the awareness or knowledge levels. In most, the participation step is especially lacking. Because we believe that participation is vital, many of the lessons in this book include ways that students can get actively involved in protecting the environment. We also realize that teachers and their students are the ones who know their own local situation best. As a result, they are the ones best able to determine what activities suggested here are most appropriate to local situations—and which ones need to be adapted to meet local needs.

Environmental Education and Current Trends in Language Education

Should language teachers stop teaching language and talk only about the environment? Definitely not. We have found that environmental education activities support language learning. For this reason, we advocate that the environment be <u>one</u> key theme in language instruction and that instructional methods actively engage students in meaningful use of language about the environment and how it can be protected. This is in line with current trends in language instruction for both native speakers and second- or foreign-language learners.

We believe that it is no coincidence that current trends in language instruction parallel changes in views of the environment. These parallels are presented in the following chart.

Trends in Views of the Environment and Language Instruction	
New Views of the Environment and their Implications	*New Trends in Instruction and their Implications*
View: Nature has the right to be active and exist independent of people. *Implications:* development of nature reserves, protection of endangered species	*View:* Students should be active. Independence should be encouraged. *Implications:* learner-centeredness, community-linked education
View: Natural diversity is recognized and encouraged. *Implications:* protection of biodiversity	*View:* Diversity among students is recognized and encouraged. *Implications:* learner-centeredness, use of methods which suit a variety of different learning styles
View: Nature exists best as an integrated whole. *Implications:* protection of the entire web of life	*View:* Students learn best when knowledge is presented as an integrated whole. *Implications:* curriculum integration, theme- or content-based instruction

Trends in Views of the Environment and Language Instruction	
New Views of the Environment and their Implications	*New Trends in Instruction and their Implications*
View: Humans are concerned about the long-term effects of production processes. *Implications*: development and use of alternative energy, reuse and recycling of materials, reduction of the amount used	*View*: Teachers are concerned about the process and long-term effects of instruction. *Implications*: emphasis on learning how to learn, developing thinking skills, and working towards intrinsic motivation
View: Humans wish to join with nature. *Implications*: increased interest in outdoor activities	*View*: Teachers wish to join with students. *Implications*: increased teacher participation in student activities and teacher modelling of the behaviors they want students to use
View: It is important for humans to cooperate with nature, not conquer it. *Implications*: efforts to live with nature without conquering it, concern over use of products made from endangered species	*View*: It is important for students to cooperate with each other, not compete. *Implications*: use of cooperative learning techniques, teaching of collaborative skills

The language lessons in the second part of this book incorporate the trends from this chart into language learning. These trends include:

— learner-centeredness;
— linking schools with the community;
— recognizing and encouraging diversity;
— integrating curriculum;
— using theme- and content-based instruction;
— teaching thinking skills;
— emphasizing the learning process;

— encouraging teacher participation; and
— encouraging cooperation.

LEARNER-CENTEREDNESS

Cognitive and humanistic theories of learning highlight the role of the learner as the key actor in the educational drama. It is the learner who is the driving force behind the success or failure of learning. Both Hugh Munby and Scott Thornbury use metaphors to contrast the teacher-centered approach with the learner-centered model. In the teacher-centered approach, the teacher is seen as the boss or owner of the classroom. Students are employees or tenants. Teachers deposit information into students' minds, which are seen as bank accounts. Teachers lead students, who follow. Teachers create activities which students use.

In the learner-centered model, teachers are seen as senior colleagues or skilled professionals who work with their junior colleagues or apprentices. Teachers and students are joint owners of the curriculum and classroom. They work as one family. Both accumulate knowledge and skills. Both work and create together. In such instruction, students take an active role in planning, preparing and carrying out learning activities. At the same time, teachers have many important roles: providing resources, models and demonstrations, organizing student learning and stimulating student thinking via questions, feedback and enrichment activities.

Comparison of Teacher-centered and Learner-centered Models		
Role of...	*Teacher-centered Model*	*Learner-centered Model*
Teacher	• boss or owner • information owner and depositor • leader • creator	• senior colleague or skilled professional • joint owner • family member • knowledge and skill accumulator • worker • creator • planner • preparer • doer

Comparison of Teacher-centered and Learner-centered Models		
Role of...	*Teacher-centered Model*	*Learner-centered Model*
		• provider of resources, models and demonstrations • learning organizer • stimulator
Students	• employees or tenants • information receivers and holders • followers • users	• junior colleagues or apprentices • joint owners • family members • knowledge and skill accumulators • workers • creators • planners • preparers • doers

LINKING SCHOOLS WITH THE COMMUNITY

As early as 1915, John Dewey advocated breaking down the walls that separate schools from the world in which students live the rest of their lives. He believed that too much of what happens in schools is artificial or isolated from the real world. School activities that involve students in the world outside the classroom promote learning. An example of such a project took place in rural Madhya Pradesh state in India between 1986 and 1988. At the time, the rural area was plagued with water-borne diseases. Secondary school students and their teachers worked together on activities that integrated school learning with community needs by collecting and analyzing water samples from common sources of drinking water. They surveyed people in the nearby communities to inform them of the project, to find out what they knew about the potential dangers of drinking polluted water and to see if people had noticed any problems which might be linked to contaminated water. Finally, students presented their findings at a public meeting.

In addition to increasing their scientific knowledge, the students improved their communication skills during the survey and presentation phases. The project generated such interest among both students and teachers that they decided to set up a volunteer environmental group to conduct activities concerned with the quality of local air, soil and water. The group is called *Neer*, the local word for water.

RECOGNIZING AND ENCOURAGING DIVERSITY

Students differ in many ways, including how they learn, what they are interested in learning, how fast they learn and the backgrounds from which they come. Educators need to consider these differences when attempting to teach. To facilitate learning, they can use a variety of techniques that appeal to different learning styles. In this way, students can benefit from methods that address their learning strengths, which may include visual, aural, kinesthetic (physical, hands-on), musical, interpersonal and individual modes of learning.

Another way of recognizing diversity is through the use of questioning. In the past, many teachers asked questions which had only one answer. Students were expected to parrot back what the teacher wanted to hear. Today, more teachers are learning to use and ask questions which have more than one possible answer. The divergent thinking required by considering such questions motivates students who already are divergent thinkers and stimulates other students to think more divergently. Such learning helps prepare students for the complexity of environmental issues. For example, when considering such issues, students may be asked to think of new uses for materials which are often thrown away. The number of 'right' answers to this question is limited only by students' imagination and experience.

INTEGRATING CURRICULUM

> *As language teachers we are the most fortunate of teachers—all subjects are ours. Whatever [the students] want to communicate about, whatever they want to read about, is our subject matter.*
>
> — Wilga Rivers, Professor of Language Education, Harvard University (1976)

Traditional classrooms break learning into separate compartments. Students learn mathematics for 50 minutes, then drop that and study language for another 50 minutes before dropping that in turn to study history. Such changes in subject matter, often accompanied by moves from one room to another, feel like changing from one television show to another. Each subject is treated as completely self-contained and unrelated to the other subjects. Learning is fragmented.

Integrated classrooms tend to use one subject area to teach many skills. The movement toward such integration comes in many forms. One example is the concept of writing across the curriculum. This has led to students using writing not only in language arts classes, but in all their courses. Writing across the curriculum is important because it develops writing skills. More importantly, it recognizes writing as an aid to developing thinking skills. As a result, language learning and learning through language become an explicit part of each course.

One way to integrate different aspects of the curriculum is for teachers to collaborate. For example, in science class students could learn about how to reduce air pollution. In language class, they could write letters to governments and companies making suggestions for cleaning the air. *Linking Mathematics and Language: Practical Classroom Activities* by Richard McCallum and Robert Whitlow provides many outstanding examples of how two seemingly diverse fields can complement each other. According to A. Ghafoor-Ghaznawi, former Chief of UNESCO's Environmental Education Unit, the environment is a holistic entity, an interconnected web of life that provides the ideal setting for curricular integration.

USING THEME- AND CONTENT-BASED INSTRUCTION

A popular means of integrating instruction is the use of theme-and content-based instruction. The twin overlapping goals of this type of instruction are to increase students' knowledge and skills in the content area at the same time as the students learn the target language. Today, most teachers attempt to provide students with many opportunities to communicate in the target language. Themes provide content for this communication.

We can bring environmental content into the classroom by choosing environmental themes. Possible themes include protection of endangered animals, air pollution, alternatives to fossil fuels and what individuals can do to save the earth. Finding materials should not be too difficult because, as the environment has become a required theme in the national curriculum of many countries, more and more environmental education materials are being produced for all ages and levels of language proficiency. Because the environment is a hot topic in the media, a great deal of very current teaching materials are available from a variety of print and electronic sources. Of course, teachers may need to adapt what they find to their students' particular needs. Most teachers already do this, no matter what the theme or curriculum.

TEACHING THINKING SKILLS

> *Creativity produces not only satisfaction and joy, it also leads to powerful consequences in our lives. It creates possibilities for solving future problems, those we cannot yet anticipate, in the coming decades.*
>
> — S.C. Utami Munandar, Chairperson, Taskforce for Gifted Education, Ministry of Education and Culture, Indonesia, and Conny Semiawan, Director, Curriculum Development Center, Ministry of Education and Culture, Indonesia (1988)

One reason for teaching thinking skills is our experience that students who do well on tests of knowledge are not able to apply their knowledge outside of test situations. What good is knowledge if we cannot use it? What good is knowledge if it doesn't help us to understand and successfully act in the varied situations we encounter during every day of our lives?

The ability to be creative is a key thinking skill. This skill consists of the following four abilities:

- fluency, the ability to generate many ideas;
- flexibility, the ability to create a wide variety of different possible solutions;
- elaboration, the ability to add on to a solution; and
- originality, the ability to generate unique and unusual solutions.

One of the best-known means of enhancing creativity and thinking skills is through the use of divergent questions. Divergent questions have many plausible alternative answers. These differ from convergent questions, which have only one right answer derived from the given information. Divergent questions encourage creativity by providing students with the freedom to generate many possible answers.

EMPHASIZING THE LEARNING PROCESS

Consistent with a learner-centered approach and efforts to enhance thinking skills is the idea that we educators should help students develop skills, strategies and attitudes needed to become life-long learners. This emphasis on teaching to promote life-long learning has led to a shift away from short-term goals. Instead of being concerned about what students can do on this week's quiz or composition assignment, teachers now coach students to become more self-sufficient by learning how to learn. When dealing with the environment, such teachers encourage students to think about the long-term effects of their actions.

The teaching of effective learning strategies helps students become more aware of how they learn and how they can improve the process. This flows from work on metacognition, which involves students consciously monitoring and regulating their own learning. Another means of encouraging life-long learning is by allowing students space to explore for themselves, make mistakes and learn from them.

ENCOURAGING TEACHER PARTICIPATION

Many educators now recognize the importance of joining with students as they experience the joys and struggles of learning. For example, when our students take out the books they have chosen for extensive reading, we read along with them from a book we enjoy. This "do-as-I-do" attitude applies to protecting the environment. When we combine classroom activities about the environment with our own environmentally-friendly actions, we model purposeful learning for our students. If the class reads about ways to reduce fossil fuel consumption, for example, we can talk about what we do in this regard. Do we take public transport to work or read books instead of watching television? If so, we point these things out to students and explain the reasons behind our lifestyle choices. We also model many of the environmentally-friendly behaviors suggested in this book's environmental lessons, thus accompanying students on their journey.

ENCOURAGING COOPERATION

Saving the environment is a task well beyond the reach of any one person acting alone. So is learning a language. Both language and environmental learning are enhanced when students help one another during the learning process. Such cooperative activities aid learning in many ways. They increase the amount of speaking each student does and generally help students to be more active, broaden the range of language that students use, create a more supportive environment for using language and increase motivation.

Outside the classroom, being able to work with others, whether in a hospital emergency room or on a committee to save a forest, demands many skills. These are the same skills that students develop by working together in the classroom to achieve common goals.

Common Questions about Integrating Environmental Education into Language Instruction

Whenever we have encouraged people to integrate environmental education and language instruction, we have been asked many questions. The following questions are the most common ones asked both by colleagues and by the people we talk to at conferences, workshops and courses. Considering our answers will assist you in understanding why we are so motivated about teaching this way.

Does integrating environmental education into language teaching mean that every lesson I do should be about the environment?

No. There are many themes that interest students and are important to them. The environment is just one of these themes.

Teaching about the environment is important, but it is not really my job. Shouldn't I stick to content such as grammar and the four skills of speaking, listening, reading and writing?

As professionals, we language educators have a role to play beyond the teaching of our particular subject. We need to examine how our work connects with the world outside the classroom. An outstanding example of an organization with such an inclusive perspective is the International Physicians for the Prevention of Nuclear War. This group was awarded the Nobel Peace Prize because its members look beyond their clinics and hospitals toward a broader definition of their professional mission. They believe that all their work will be for nothing if their patients die in a nuclear war.

People from a wide range of professions have developed similar integrated views of their callings. In the field of education, there are many local, national and international organizations in which people volunteer their time and expertise. Language educators are no exception to this trend. In Japan, for example, language educators established the Global Issues in Language Education Network. (For more information, contact Professor Kip Cates, Tottori University, Koyama, Tottori City 680, Japan.) Columbia University's master's degree program in Teaching English to Speakers of Other Languages now includes a global issues course.

In today's increasingly interconnected and interdependent world, we language education professionals must see our task as more than one of preparing students to pass examinations. We are preparing students for citizenship in their communities, nations, regions and the world. The following poem by Tim Newfields, an English teacher in Japan, captures this spirit. It first appeared in the newsletter of the Global Issues in Language Education Network.

The Flavor of Apathy

I am eating a bowl of ice cream
as bullets scream
around the world.
I am scooping out a big strawberry
as forest after forest
vanishes in smoke.
I am biting into another scoop
as fear and hatred
spread like germs across the earth.
I am licking my spoon after the last bite
as the vacant eyes of hungry children
force me to question:
Just how sweet is the taste of indifference?

— Tim J. Newfields

I've already got so much to teach that I can't finish the syllabus. If I add stuff about the environment, I'll be even further behind.

One trend in language instruction is teaching language via content or themes. In this way, students learn language in the course of using it to speak, listen, read and write about particular content. Content becomes the vehicle by which language is learned. The focus is on meaning rather than form.

This does not mean that form is unimportant. Instead of learning specific features of the English language in isolation, however, students study these features in the context of an overall focus on meaning and content. The theory is that this type of instruction promotes learning and is better understood than an exclusive focus on the elements of language. By following this methodology, teachers can use the same syllabus to handle many skills, including language and environmental ones. In this way, students are more likely to learn the language skills that they cover.

That sounds nice, and I agree with it philosophically, but my students have to prepare for standardized tests. If they don't do well, everyone—administrators, parents, students and I—will be very unhappy.

Again, the belief is that a focus on content and meaning—in this case concerning the environment—will promote learning better than form-focused instruction. There is research to support this belief. Further, we have to consider whether standardized tests are measuring what is important or only what is easy to measure on standardized tests. Many countries, international bodies and individual citizens are urging that learning about the environment is an important part of education and should be part of the evaluation process. As was mentioned in the introduction, learning does not equal wisdom: many of the people responsible for environmental destruction hold university degrees. If we believe that environmental education is important, we need to take a stand by teaching the skills necessary for environmental action. Language class is an excellent place for teaching such skills.

I'm very weak in science. How can I possibly teach about the environment?

We all need to understand about the environment in order to protect it effectively; however, everyone, including the top scientists, still has a lot to learn. There are several things we teachers can do to increase our knowledge:

- We can work with science teachers. This is one way to promote curricular integration.
- We can invite people from the community with special knowledge about the environment to speak to our classes.
- We can learn from and with our students. It's okay for us to admit that we don't know everything about the environment.
- We can go out and learn about the environment, then share our new knowledge with our students. Such behavior

models concerned engagement with the environment for our students.

To help us with all of these steps, many companies are creating print, video and computer materials on environmental issues. These materials are available at all levels of language ability and scientific knowledge.

I like the lessons in this book; how can I get more?

The best way to get more environmental lessons is to use the ones here as models for developing some of your own. In doing this, consider the two main ways that we developed the lessons in this book.

— We took an English teaching method we liked and put some environmental content into it. One example of this type of activity is the lesson on developing an environmental questionnaire. Questionnaires are one of many ways of creating an information gap between students. An information gap refers to information that one or more students have that others do not have. To complete an assigned task, students need to close the gap by communicating with one another. To give the questionnaire an environmental slant, we wrote questionnaire items related to what people do regarding the environment. Consider adding environmental content to your favorite language technique. Any technique that is good for teaching language is good for integrating the environment into language instruction.

— We started with a theme or a text about the environment, then thought about a language activity that could go with it. That was how the lesson on understanding diagrams was created. We wanted to talk about treating waste water. We found a diagram in a brochure by the Singapore Ministry of Environment that we thought illustrated this well. We dug into our bag of teaching techniques and decided to focus a lesson on listening skills. We built in an information gap by creating different versions of the diagram, each missing some information. To learn about waste water treatment, students have to ask each other questions. They then apply what they have learned by considering how they can help reduce the amount and toxicity of waste water.

Don't worry about creating all of your own lessons. Why not share with others? Share with teachers at your school, through professional organizations, journals and conferences and by contacting environmental organizations. Many environmental organizations have education departments where staff and volunteers love to hear about successful environmental activities. Many have also developed environmental materials and activities for school use.

Lesson Format

The lessons in this book include some or all of the elements shown in the chart below.

Explanation of Lesson Format	
Lesson Element	*Purpose*
Introduction	Provides background on the lesson's instructional technique or environmental focus.
Environmental Focus	Includes environmental education objectives and aspects of the environment brought up in the lesson.
Language Focus	Provides suggestions about an aspect of language which can be examined and practiced in the lesson. This involves such things as grammar, functions, vocabulary and text structure. Some teachers will wish to spend a lot of time on this; others will opt for a less explicit approach.
Language Skills	Outlines the main language skills practiced, including speaking, listening, reading and writing.
Time	Provides an estimate of how long the lesson will take.
Materials	Includes a list of materials teachers need for the activity. Where necessary, this section also provides answer keys.
Preparation	Outlines what teachers need to do ahead of the language class. This includes preparing handouts and organizing materials.

Explanation of Lesson Format	
Procedure	Offers recommendations about how to teach the lesson.
Variations	Makes suggestions about additional ways to use the procedure or ways to vary it.
Language Corner	Provides explicit guidance on a point of language use.

Ideas To Facilitate Group Discussions

There are many different ways for groups to function, many strategies that help to keep the group focused and a variety of methods to ensure that all members are able to participate. Some useful methods and strategies are detailed below. They will be referred to in the procedures part of the various lessons.

COLLABORATIVE SKILLS

In order to collaborate, students need to learn how to encourage each other to participate. This is an important skill for several reasons:

- For groups to achieve their goals, everyone needs to participate.
- Students who do not participate may not support decisions the group makes; making decisions collaboratively encourages group cohesion.
- Individuals show that they value others' ideas by encouraging them to participate.

There are many ways to encourage others to participate. The chart below gives some examples of what collaboration can look like and sound like. In order to feel more comfortable with using these techniques, groups of students might role-play some of the techniques. They can then practice them during group activities.

Encouraging Others to Participate	
Looks Like	*Sounds Like*
Smiling	What do you think?
Sitting close together and looking at the person you are addressing	I'd like to know what you think.
Looking at the person you are inviting to speak	We haven't heard from you yet. What's your opinion?
Showing interest in what others say by nodding your head, leaning towards them, etc.	Would you mind sharing your opinion with us?

GROUP ROLES

Groups function well when all members have a role to play. Some students may feel more comfortable in some roles than others. In order to become proficient group workers, however, they need to learn to recognize and perform all group roles. This can be facilitated by having students maintain the same groups for several activities. They can then rotate roles at the beginning of a new activity. Alternatively, students can be encouraged to volunteer to perform a role that they have not yet tried. Some important group roles are outlined in the following chart.

Group Roles	
Role	*Function*
Recorder	The recorder ensures that the group's ideas are recorded. This may take the form of a written report, chart, picture or diagram.
Encourager	The encourager ensures that all members participate. This person watches body language, then uses both verbal and non-verbal techniques to draw out the silent participants and ensure that no one person monopolizes the discussion.

Group Roles	
Role	*Function*
Timekeeper	The timekeeper urges the group to keep within the prescribed time limits. If the group is spending too much time on one aspect of the task, the timekeeper may have to move the group along to another part.
Reporter	The reporter briefly shares the group's discussions with the larger group or class.

JIGSAW

This group technique uses the knowledge of certain group members to teach other group members a specific skill or piece of information. Although there are several ways to use the jigsaw technique, the following steps are the most common:

1. Divide the class into *home teams*. Each home team consists of four students.
2. Provide each member of the home team with information, such as a magazine article on a different aspect of the same topic. To simplify differentiating between the various articles, number them #1, #2, #3 and #4.
3. Have team members look at the number on their article, then leave their home team to form *expert teams* with other students who have the same article.
4. The expert team's job is to work together until each member in the expert team understands the material well enough to present it to the home team. You may ask expert team members to present their knowledge to their group in a specific way. For example, you might ask them to make a chart or develop a mind map.
5. Once the expert teams have collaborated, ask members to return to their original home teams. Each home team now has four different people with expertise in one aspect of the topic. Members can take turns sharing the information they learned in the expert teams.
6. The group then does a task or takes a quiz based on information from each of the group members.

TAKING TURNS

To facilitate discussion, students can be encouraged to take turns speaking, one after the other, around their group of four. This helps quieter students to participate and prevents one or two people from monopolizing the discussion. Although this technique is useful, it is important not to pressure those who are not ready to speak. Such students should be encouraged, by smiles and positive comments, to participate at another time.

. . . .

ENVIRONMENTAL LESSONS

Sounds in the Environment

INTRODUCTION

This lesson concerns the sounds we hear around us. We hope that students will learn to appreciate the beauty of natural sounds. We also want to make students aware of noise pollution, its sources and ways of diminishing it. In urban areas, noise pollution is a problem because it damages the ears and stresses the nervous system. This is true for humans and animals. In natural settings, noise pollution can also interfere with the reproductive cycles of certain species.

ENVIRONMENTAL FOCUS

awareness and participation—awareness of sounds, noise pollution

LANGUAGE FOCUS

past progressive, writing stories

LANGUAGE SKILLS

listening, writing

TIME

Part 1: 10-15 minutes
Part 2: 30-40 minutes
Part 3: 20-25 minutes

MATERIALS

one piece of used notebook paper per student
tape recorders (optional)
Teacher Script: One Evening at Home

PREPARATION

Practice reading the story outlined under "Teacher Script" below. You may wish to tape-record it.

Teacher Script: One Evening At Home

One evening, a family was sitting outside talking. (*Stop and make a talking sound.*)
They were talking and laughing. (*Make a laughing sound.*)
There were a lot of animals around. The lizards were clicking their tongues. (*Click your tongue.*)
The frogs were making their sound too. (*Ribbit, ribbit, ribbit.*)
There were also some mice. (*Squeak, squeak, squeak.*)
The wind was blowing stronger and stronger. (*Whistle or rub your palms together.*)
The leaves on the trees were shaking. (*Place the palms of your hands on each side of a paper and shake it back and forth.*)
Then a light rain started to fall. (*Tap your fingers gently on a desk.*)
Soon, the family heard thunder. (*Loudly clap your hands.*)
Heavy rain came down. (*Slap your hands on your thighs or on a desk.*)
Everyone got up and ran into the house. (*Stamp your feet.*)

PROCEDURE

Part 1

1. (*Whole class*) Students sit in a circle.
2. (*Whole class*) Teacher tells the story outlined in the script, possibly writing key words on the board.
3. (*Whole class*) When a sound is mentioned in the story, teacher makes the sound, then, one at a time, each student around the circle makes the sound. Directions for making the sound are in parentheses in the "Teacher Script."
4. (*Whole class*) In preparation for Part 2, students discuss how the past progressive tense is used in the story. (See "Language Corner.")

Part 2

1. (*Individual*) Outside school, students listen for sounds, both pleasant and unpleasant. These can be natural or human-made. Students can tape-record the sounds or practice imitating them.
2. (*Groups*) In the next class, groups of students make up their own stories using the sounds they gathered for homework.
3. (*Whole class*) Groups perform their stories for the rest of the class. Group members take turns reading sections of their stories and making the required sounds.

Part 3

1. (*Whole class*) Discussion of noise pollution: What is it? What causes it? Why is it a concern? How can it be prevented?
2. (*Whole class*) Students identify sources of noise pollution in their communities.
3. (*Groups*) In groups, students choose one or more sources of noise pollution and make a plan outlining what they can do to reduce the pollution. Each group member should have a role to play in carrying out the plan. For example, if there is a noisy construction project in the neighborhood, group members might divide their work into four tasks. One might go to the library to read about what can be done to reduce noise pollution around construction sites. Another might talk to construction workers to find out how they cope with high noise levels. A third might write a letter of complaint to the construction company, and a fourth might write to the local government.

LANGUAGE CORNER: PAST PROGRESSIVE

One of the purposes of the past progressive tense is to talk about actions which continue for some time in the past. This tense is formed by combining the past tense of the verb *to be* with the present participle: verb + ing.

Structure: past tense of *to be* + present participle

Example: The wind *was blowing*.
The leaves *were shaking*.

Some verbs, such as *to hear* and *to see*, do not usually take past progressive forms.

Green Gifts

INTRODUCTION

This activity develops and fosters group cohesion and collaboration by having students discuss and reflect on how well they are working together. To accomplish this, students make a gift from recycled materials, then present the gift and a note of thanks to a fellow group member.

ENVIRONMENTAL FOCUS

skills and participation—reusing resources

LANGUAGE FOCUS

gerunds

LANGUAGE SKILLS

speaking, writing

TIME

40 minutes

MATERIALS

used materials that can be made into gifts

PREPARATION

Bring in some used materials that can be made into gifts. These can include used bottles, cans, straws and newspapers. Either make a sample gift from some of the used items or show an example made by a student.

PROCEDURE

1. (*Whole class*) Students discuss how gifts can be made from materials that are often thrown away. Students will likely have many ideas. For example, they can cut plastic drink bottles into different shapes, such as birds. They can make sculptures and key chains from old straws. They can make envelopes from used paper or paint used jars to make attractive containers.
2. (*Individual*) Students receive the name of one person with whom they have been working. They keep the name of this person secret.
3. (*Individual*) At home or in art class, students make a present from reused materials.

4. (*Whole class*) Teacher explains what a gerund is and works with students to develop a list of gerunds that could be used in thank-you notes. (See "Language Corner.") Teacher and students develop a second list of thanking phrases students can use to provide variety in their sentences. Such structures and phrases include the following:
   - You listened carefully when I talked. Thanks. (past tense)
   - You made sure our team didn't waste time. (past tense)
   - What a great teammate you are! (present tense)
   - You're terrific! You helped me understand. (present tense)
5. (*Individual*) Students individually prepare notes thanking the person named in #2. Students specifically mention examples of collaborative behavior.
6. (*Groups*) Students exchange gifts and notes in class.

VARIATIONS

1. Students who have made something unique describe how they made their present.
2. Before a holiday, students discuss presents they will make from reused materials. In class, students prepare notes to accompany the presents. The notes explain that the present is made from reused materials in an effort to protect the environment.
3. Students make unusual items for sale at a school event. Proceeds go to an environmental club or organization.

LANGUAGE CORNER: GERUNDS

Gerunds are verbs which act like nouns. Usually, gerunds refer to an action which is already happening or has been completed. They also suggest that action is continuous. Gerunds are formed by adding -ing to the infinitive: Listen-ing.

Structure: infinitive of verb + *-ing*

Example: *Studying* with you has been great fun.
I enjoy *hearing* your jokes.
Thank you for *asking* me questions about my composition.
Thank you for *listening* to me when I gave my point of view.
Working with you was really great because you are a good listener.
I enjoyed *listening* to your ideas.

Dialogue Journals

INTRODUCTION

Dialogue journals are one way of encouraging students to use writing as a tool for thinking and for communicating with others. Ideas, feelings, information, events, opinions and actions related to the environment provide fertile ground for such thought and communication.

ENVIRONMENTAL FOCUS

awareness and participation

LANGUAGE FOCUS

writing with a focus on content and thinking

LANGUAGE SKILLS

writing, reading

TIME

20-30 minutes

MATERIALS

Blackline Master: Guidelines for Writing Environment Journals

PREPARATION

Make one copy of Blackline Master: Guidelines for Environmental Journals for each student. Students can refer to these guidelines when writing their journal entries

PROCEDURE

1. (*Whole class*) Teacher distributes and discusses the guidelines for writing environment journals.
2. (*Individual*) Students bring a notebook to school to use as a journal. Alternatively, they can make a journal from paper used only on one side. These journals can be stored in the classroom.
3. (*Individual*) In their own time, students can take trips to nature reserves, read articles about the environment and learn about

or participate in actions to protect the environment. These experiences provide ideas for journal entries. (See "Language Corner.")

4. (*Pairs*) After writing, students exchange journals with a partner. Partners read each other's latest entry. They then write a response in their partner's journal and sign their names. Teachers might like to suggest encouraging and positive words students can include in their responses.
5. (*Teacher*) Teacher keeps a journal and also exchanges with students. In this way, the teacher provides a model of how to write entries and provide feedback.

VARIATIONS

1. Journal entries can be printed at home and pasted into journals. In this case, journals can be made of paper used on both sides.
2. Student ideas about a particular topic can be edited and collated into a newsletter.
3. Selected teacher and student entries can be read to or by the whole class.

LANGUAGE CORNER: WRITING WITH A FOCUS ON CONTENT AND THINKING

Journal entries should not be edited for grammar, spelling or punctuation; however, teacher analysis of the mistakes and miscues in these entries can provide ideas for future language lessons. Some teachers occasionally provide short mini-lessons at the beginning of journal writing time. These mini-lessons revolve around language areas with which several students are having difficulty.

Journals can provide a starting point for other writing activities. For example, ideas generated in the journals can be used as a base to write a letter or an article about a particular environmental issue. After such writing has been revised for content and students are happy with their ideas, the focus can shift to matters which are ignored when writing journal entries. These include grammar, spelling and punctuation.

Guidelines for Environment Journals

1. The purpose of the journal is to give you a chance to exchange ideas, information and feelings on topics, events and actions related to the environment. You can write on any topic that has some connection to the environment.

2. Your classmates and I will read your journal entries and respond to them. Please leave space for us to make comments. You can do this by writing on every other line, leaving big margins or leaving space at the end.

3. Write a minimum of _______ words. This will give you a chance to develop and explain your topic.

4. Be sure that your name is on your journal. Each entry should have a date and title.

5. Do not worry about grammar, spelling or punctuation. The focus of journals is on expressing your ideas.

6. You can use pen, typewriter or computer to prepare your journal. If you use handwriting, be sure to write legibly.

What's in the Packaging?

INTRODUCTION

Products are packaged in many ways. In this activity, students will group packaging into one of three categories. Biodegradable packages are those that will break down naturally. Fruits and nuts such as walnuts, oranges and bananas come with biodegradable peels or shells. Although little manufactured packaging is biodegradable, some of it is easy to recycle or reuse. This includes paper and plastic shopping bags and glass bottles. Unfortunately, many commercial products come with large amounts of unnecessary packaging, such as plastic bubble packing and Styrofoam. These materials are more difficult to recycle and reuse. In this activity, students focus their attention on the decisions they make as consumers. This involves many important thinking skills, including the following:

- categorizing, comparing and contrasting;
- identifying cause and effect relationships;
- giving reasons; and
- evaluating.

The activity will be more real if students investigate what recycling programs exist in their area. This will differ from place to place. Keep in mind that different items can be classified differently depending on the situation and the individual student's interpretation. Accept students' classifications if they can explain the reason for their classifications.

ENVIRONMENTAL FOCUS

ability and participation—being a green consumer

LANGUAGE FOCUS

similarity, difference

LANGUAGE SKILLS

writing, speaking, listening

TIME

Part 1: 10-15 minutes
Part 2: 25-30 minutes

MATERIALS

examples of the following types of waste packaging: nutshells, orange peels, banana peels, paper or plastic shopping bags, glass bottles, plastic bubble packing, Styrofoam containers, plastic wrapping

Teacher Example: Sample Packaging Table

Blackline Master: What's in the Packaging?

Teacher Example: Sample Packaging Table

Example	*Is this the way it occurs in nature?*	*Is this easy to recycle or reuse?*	*Source?*	*Purpose?*	*Is this necessary?*
orange peel	yes	no	orange tree	to protect the fruit	yes
paper bag	no	yes	trees	to protect purchases, to carry things	sometimes
Styrofoam	no	no	petroleum	to keep food	no, we can use reusable containers

PREPARATION

Part 1: Bring in different types of waste packaging. Make a large blank copy of Blackline Master: What's in the Packaging? Use it to show students how to categorize sample packaging materials.

Part 2: Make and distribute one copy of Blackline Master: What's in the Packaging? for each group of three students.

PROCEDURE

Part 1

1. (*Whole class*) Students discuss the three types of packaging (biodegradable, recyclable, reusable) and look at examples of each. Students identify the source of each type of packaging and decide whether or not it is necessary.
2. (*Whole class*) Students work together to develop and fill in a class chart similar to the sample table under "Teacher Example: Sample Packaging Table."
3. (*Individual*) For the next week, students save types of packaging to bring to school.

Part 2

1. (*Whole class*) Students review the vocabulary describing the different types of packaging and how to fill out the packaging chart.
2. (*Groups*) In groups of three, students use the packaging which group members brought to school in filling in Blackline Master: What's in the Packaging?
3. (*Individual*) Students write sentences comparing and contrasting packaging which is necessary with that which is unnecessary. (See "Language Corner" for examples that may be helpful.) Students speculate on why the unnecessary packaging is used. For example, does it make the product look nicer or prevent theft?
4. (*Groups*) One at a time, students discuss how they, their families and businesses might be able to reduce the amount of packaging they use. Students also explain what they already do to use less packaging.
5. (*Whole class*) Students and teacher share their good ideas. To promote attentive listening, students share their group mates' ideas rather than their own.

VARIATIONS

1. In groups, students develop radio commercials and posters to disseminate their suggestions about reducing packaging. Stu-

dents look for opportunities to present their ideas to other classes, at other schools or to community groups.

2. Students discuss whether protecting the environment depends mostly on what individuals do or what governments and big companies do.

LANGUAGE CORNER: SIMILARITY AND DIFFERENCE

There are various structures that students can use in discussing similarities and differences. The structures below will assist them.

Similarity

Structure 1: Statement about Item 1 + *similarly* + statement about Item 2

Example: The purpose of an orange peel is to protect the fruit. *Similarly,* the purpose of a paper bag is to protect the things we buy.

Structure 2: Item 1 and Item 2 + *both* + statement of how they are similar

Example: Orange peels and paper bags *both* come from nature.

Difference

Structure 1: Statement about Item 1 + *but* + statement about Item 2

Example: Orange peels are necessary, *but* sometimes paper bags are not necessary.

Structure 2: *While* + statement about Item 1 + statement about Item 2.

Example: *While* paper bags are easily reused, Styrofoam containers are not.

What's in the Packaging?

Packaging: Where does it come from? How is it used?

Example	*Is this the way it occurs in nature?*	*Is this easy to recycle or reuse?*	*Source?*	*Purpose?*	*Is this necessary?*

Do an Energy Audit!

INTRODUCTION

Students' homes can be good places for them to learn about the environment and how to protect it. One way to encourage such learning is to ask students to audit their family's use of resources. Such audits can later be expanded to include the homes of relatives and neighbors, as well as schools, shops and business offices.

ENVIRONMENTAL FOCUS

skills and participation—energy use

LANGUAGE FOCUS

modals

TIME

30 minutes, with a lot of work done at home

MATERIALS

Teacher Script: What Is an Energy Audit?
Blackline Master: Sample Energy Audit Table
Blackline Master: Home Energy Audit

Teacher Script: What is an Audit?

An audit is an examination or investigation of something. In this activity, you are going to audit the amount of energy your family uses. There are many ways we use energy. Watching television uses electricity. Driving a car uses gasoline or petrol. Using a calculator uses battery or solar power.

An Energy Audit Table can be used to do an energy audit. Here's how to use such a table.

- In the first column, write the name of an item that uses energy. This includes televisions, cars and calculators.
- In the second column, write the number of these items your family has.
- In the third column, indicate the source of energy used.
- In the fourth column, show how many hours per week your family uses the item.

- In the last column, list what alternatives there are to using the item. To answer this, consider what you would do if you did not have the item. Include alternatives that you like and ones that you do not like.

PREPARATION

Make an overhead transparency of Blackline Master: Sample Energy Audit Table.
Make one copy of Blackline Master: Home Energy Audit for each student.

PROCEDURE

1. (*Whole class*) Teacher explains what an energy audit is and describes how to do one. Students discuss the sample energy audit table. Teacher makes sure that everyone understands the various parts of the table.
2. (*Individual*) Students do their own home energy audit. On the back of the energy audit sheet, they write answers to the following questions:

   a) How many people live in your home?
   b) How much is your typical energy bill per month?
      Remind students to include electricity, gasoline or petrol, batteries and any other power sources. For example, families who pay $45 for electricity, $25 for gasoline or petrol and $8 for batteries spend $78 a month on energy.
   c) On the average, how much energy does each person living in your home use in one month?
      Have students calculate this by dividing the total of their monthly energy bill by the number of people in the household.
   d) How could you save energy?
      Before discussing answers to this question, introduce the modals outlined in the "Language Corner." Provide several models of how students might respond to such a question.

3. (*Pairs*) Students share their audits and the answers to the questions with a partner. Partners check each other's work for completeness. They then sign each other's tables as checkers.

4. (*Individual*) Partners compare their findings and write a paragraph explaining how their individual findings differed from those of their partner.
5. (*Whole class*) For questions 2 (a), 2 (b) and 2 (c), students compute the class average so that they can learn more about energy use in their classmates' homes. In order to encourage partner discussion, students report their partner's ideas for 2 (d).
6. (*Individual*) Teacher reminds students to use such phrases as *I could, I might, I will* or *We can*.
7. Students and their families implement measures to reduce energy use. Students do another home audit at a later date to see if the measures have been effective.

VARIATIONS

1. Students discuss the sources of the energy they use. Electricity, for example, could come from non-renewable resources such as coal and petroleum or renewable resources such as solar or wind power.
2. Students do an energy audit of the school.
3. Students do an audit of water use or garbage generation.
4. Students learn how to read electric meters and the energy efficiency ratings of appliances.

LANGUAGE CORNER: MODALS

Modals are words which show the attitude of the speaker toward the condition or action described in the sentence. *Could* is a modal. Other modals include: *can, may, might, will* and *would*. Modals are often followed by the infinitive form of a verb without using *to*. Also, modals do not change form to agree with the subject.

Structure: modal + infinitive of verb without *to*

Example: My brother *could buy* rechargable batteries for his flashlight.
We *can reduce* our energy bill.
My friend *may decide* to buy a solar-powered calculator.
My parents *might be* able to take public transport to work instead of driving a car.
I *will watch* less television next week.
You *would use* less energy if you walked to school.

Sample Energy Audit Table

Item	*Number*	*Power Source*	*Usage in Hours per Week*	*Alternatives*
TV	2	electricity	28	read more, get more exercise, talk to people more
car	1	gasoline, petrol	10	walk, ride a bike, take a bus, carry heavy things
calculator	2	batteries	6	calculate by hand, get a solar-powered calculator

Home Energy Audit

Name : ______________________________

Checker : ______________________________

Item	*Number*	*Power Source*	*Usage in Hours per Week*	*Alternatives*

Conduct An Environmental Survey!

INTRODUCTION

Environmental concerns are often presented as someone else's problem. This activity helps students to see how they can play a direct role in improving the environment. Awareness leads to action. Students might extend the activity by discussing what they currently are doing to help the environment, then planning ways they could work together on such activities.

Students and teachers are free to disagree with the scoring of the questionnaire. Discussing alternative scoring exercises evaluative skills.

ENVIRONMENTAL FOCUS

awareness and participation—environmentally-friendly behaviors

LANGUAGE FOCUS

conditional words

LANGUAGE SKILLS

reading, listening

TIME

1 hour

MATERIALS

Blackline Master: Do You Care about the Environment?
Blackline Master: Scoring Key

PREPARATION

Print one copy of Blackline Master: Do You Care about the Environment? for each pair of students. Laminate copies so that they can be reused with another group.

Make an overhead transparency of Blackline Master: Scoring Key.

PROCEDURE

1. (*Whole class*) Teacher introduces vocabulary and structures that may be unfamiliar to students. Students discuss unfamiliar vocabulary and structures. For example, they might need to know that ivory comes from elephants' tusks and what a slaughterhouse and a rally are. In addition, see "Language Corner" for information on the conditional.
2. (*Pairs*) Students work in pairs with one copy of the questionnaire per pair. Each student writes on a piece of paper the numbers 1-10, followed by a, b and c next to each number. One student then reads aloud the first question. Both students write down their answers. The second student then reads out the second question and both students write down their answers. Students continue to read alternate questions.
3. (*Pairs*) As they do each item, students discuss their answers with each other and explain the reasons for their choices.
4. (*Whole class*) Students check their answers with the scoring key and discuss their results. Teachers encourage students to disagree with the scoring key by asking the following questions:

   - What do you think of the questionnaire?
   - Do you think that the scoring is fair?
   - Do you have your own choices of action that are not included on the questionnaire?

   If students can provide good reasons, adjust the scoring key according to their suggestions.

VARIATIONS

1. Students can write two or more questions to add to the questionnaire and prepare a scoring key for their new questions. Teacher encourages conditional questions such as "What would happen if you (+ past tense)?"
2. Students in pairs or groups read texts or look at pictures which demonstrate behavior that is friendly and unfriendly to the environment. They then prepare a questionnaire for another group.
3. Students discuss what part they can play in protecting the environment and suggest activities to promote this. For example, students prepare posters or flyers to distribute around the school community.

4. Instead of filling in the questionnaire, students brainstorm possible answers, then develop their own scoring key.

LANGUAGE CORNER: CONDITIONAL

The questionnaire uses the conditional to talk about an unreal or imaginary situation. One way to form the conditional is shown below.

Structure: *If* + past tense of verb + *would* + infinitive without *to*
Example 1: *If* you *lost* your wallet, what would you do?
Example 2: *If* you won a thousand dollars, how much *would* you *give* to an environmental organization?

To teach the conditional form, choose one or two of the questions from the questionnaire. Elicit full-sentence answers using prompts.

Teacher: If you had to go to a place which was about two miles (kilometres) away, how would you choose to travel?
Prompt 1: I would...
Prompt 2: Show pictures of the following methods of transportation:
[sketch of a car] go by car
[sketch of feet] walk
[sketch of a train] take the train

To assist students in asking each other conditional questions, provide a prompt card with the following script:

Structure: *If* ... [past tense verb] ... *how* ... *would* + infinitive of verb without *to* ...?
Example: *If* you *wanted* to help the environment, *how would* you *do* it?

Do You Care about the Environment?

Do this questionnaire with your partner and see how well you rate as people who care about the environment!

1. If you had to go to a place which was about two miles (kilometres) away, how would you choose to travel?
   (a) by car?
   (b) on foot?
   (c) by bus?

2. If you were traveling on a train and bought some food, what would you do with the food wrapper?
   (a) Put it in your bag to dispose of later?
   (b) Throw it on the floor for the cleaners to pick up?
   (c) Throw it out of the window?

3. If you purchased items that were packed in a plastic bag, what would you do with the bag?
   (a) Save it to use as a household rubbish bag?
   (b) Throw it away?
   (c) Use it as many times as possible for various uses?

4. If you were filling a large bucket of water when the telephone rang, what would you do?
   (a) Turn off the water before answering the telephone?
   (b) Go straight to the phone without turning off the water because it could be an urgent call?
   (c) Slow down the flow of water and go to the phone?

5. If you heard about a 'Save the Trees' rally being held at a logging company's office, what would you do?
   (a) Watch out for news of the rally?
   (b) Forget about it since you are not responsible for cutting down trees?
   (c) Find out how to take part in similar rallies?

6. If you saw a caged monkey in a shop or market, what would you do?
   (a) Buy it to keep at home?
   (b) Think it was very cute?
   (c) Tell the seller about how cruel it is to cage wild animals?

7. If you saw some lambs being packed into a truck to be taken to the slaughterhouse, what would you do?
   (a) Want to cry and decide to find a way to help the lambs?
   (b) Be surprised that so many lambs can be packed into one truck?
   (c) Feel hungry?

8. If you gave your best friend a present, which of the following would you choose?
   (a) an ivory pendant?
   (b) a leather bag?
   (c) a present you made yourself from reused materials?

9. If you found out that a factory was pouring poisonous chemicals into a river, what would you do?
   (a) Avoid buying that company's products?
   (b) Remind yourself that the poison will get washed into the sea?
   (c) Write letters to the company, newspapers and government bodies?

10. If you discovered that there was a rat in your house, what would you do?
   (a) Get a cat?
   (b) Kill it with a stone or stick?
   (c) Put out rat poison?

Scoring Key

Check your answers with the scores below. Give yourself the number of points next to your answer, then total up your points.

1.	(a) -2	(b) 2	(c) 1
2.	(a) 1	(b) -1	(c) -2
3.	(a) 1	(b) -1	(c) 2
4.	(a) 2	(b) -2	(c) 1
5.	(a) 0	(b) -2	(c) 2
6.	(a) -2	(b) -2	(c) 2
7.	(a) 2	(b) -1	(c) -2
8.	(a) -2	(b) -1	(c) 1
9.	(a) 1	(b) -2	(c) 2
10.	(a) 2	(b) -1	(c) -2

Less than -10

You need to become environmentally aware. It is time to start reading and learning about the environment.

-3 to -9

You have some basic understanding of the environment and what needs to be done to protect it. Perhaps until now you haven't realized the part you yourself can play. Now is the time to change. Read everything you can about saving our natural resources.

-2 to 3

You are obviously concerned about the environment and you are clearly taking action to preserve it. Keep up the good work and find out what else you can do to make a difference.

4 to 9

Very good. You are doing a lot to help the environment. Where can you improve?

10 or higher

Excellent! It is a shame everyone isn't as concerned as you are. Help to educate those around you who know less than you. Continue to keep up with what you can do to help.

No matter what your score is, keep learning about ways to protect the environment. There won't be another one if we allow it to disappear!

Understanding Diagrams

INTRODUCTION

Diagrams help to clarify the steps in many processes, both in the natural and in the human world. They also help students to see the interconnectedness of different elements. In this activity, students cooperate to gather all the information required to understand a diagram on waste water.

ENVIRONMENTAL FOCUS

knowledge and participation—waste water

LANGUAGE FOCUS

passive voice

SKILLS

speaking, writing

TIME

30-40 minutes

MATERIALS

Blackline Master: Activity Sheet #1—Disposal of Waste Water
Blackline Master: Activity Sheet #2—Disposal of Waste Water
Blackline Master: Activity Sheet #3—Disposal of Waste Water
Blackline Master: Answer Key

PREPARATION

Prepare one set of the three activity sheets for each group of three students.
Make an overhead transparency of Blackline Master: Answer Key.

PROCEDURE

1. (*Whole class*) Teacher finds out how much students know about what is done with waste water and how it is treated. See "Language Corner" for use of the passive voice during this discussion.

2. (*Groups*) Students form groups of three and number themselves #1, #2 and #3.
3. (*Groups*) Group members receive versions of the activity sheet that correlate with their numbers.
4. (*Groups*) The student with Activity Sheet #1 tells the others about the information on this diagram. Then the students with Activity Sheets #2 and #3 provide the information on their diagrams. Teacher may provide the following prompts:

   Prompt: In my diagram I have blanks at the top of the page.

   Response: I have something there. It says...

   All three members of the group fill in the information missing on their diagrams.
5. (*Groups*) After students share the information from each diagram, they use the labeled diagrams in completing the sentences above each diagram. They then put the sentences into the correct order. Each group then checks their responses with the teacher or answer key.
6. (*Whole class*) Students review the contents of the diagram by asking themselves various questions prompted by the teacher.

   Prompt 1: Where does waste water come from? (from apartments, from industries, etc.)
   Prompt 2: What substances does the water contain? (detergents, chemicals, etc.)
7. (*Groups*) Students compile a report on the different substances in waste water and explain how each harms the environment. The report should end with recommendations on what students think they can do to cut down on the amount of waste water and what they can do to reduce the amount of harmful substances. These statements might use the conditional phrases learned in "Environmental Questionnaire."

VARIATIONS

1. Teachers may wish to pre-teach relevant phrases and words, such as waste water and treatment. They might also teach the following three related words:

   sewers (underground pipes);

sewage (the waste water that flows into the sewers); and *sewerage* (the process of treating sewage).

2. The exercise is good preparation for research into waste water. One way to investigate the subject is to have a field trip to a local waterworks unit.
3. Students prepare posters advising people on how to conserve water.
4. Students construct their own diagrams showing a particular process relevant to the environment, plus human impact on that process.

LANGUAGE CORNER: PASSIVE VOICE

The passive voice makes the object of an action the subject of the sentence. It is used to describe processes when people want to focus on the process rather than the people who manage the process.

Structure: object of action + appropriate form of *to be* + past participle of verb

Example: The *water* (object) *was poured* down the sink by Peter.

Compare this with the equivalent active sentence: Peter poured the water down the sink.

The diagrams in this activity contain examples of processes that can be described using both active and passive sentences. Examples such as the ones below can be used to contrast the two forms.

Active

People in apartments, restaurants, industries and other places dispose of waste water.
The waste water flows into the sewers. The sewers flow underground toward the pumping station.

Passive

The *waste water* in the sewers *is pumped* from the pumping station to the sewage treatment works.
At the sewage treatment works, the *waste water is* partially *cleaned*.
The *treated water is pumped* out into the sea.

Activity Sheet #1—Disposal of Waste Water

The sewerage system is for the disposal of waste water.
The waste water in the sewers is pumped from the p_______________ s_______________ to the s_______________ t_______________ w_______________.
The treated water is pumped out into the s__________.
Waste water from a_______________, r_______________, i_______________ and other places goes into s_______________.
At the s_______________ t_______________ works, the waste water is partially cleaned.
The sewers flow underground toward the pumping station.

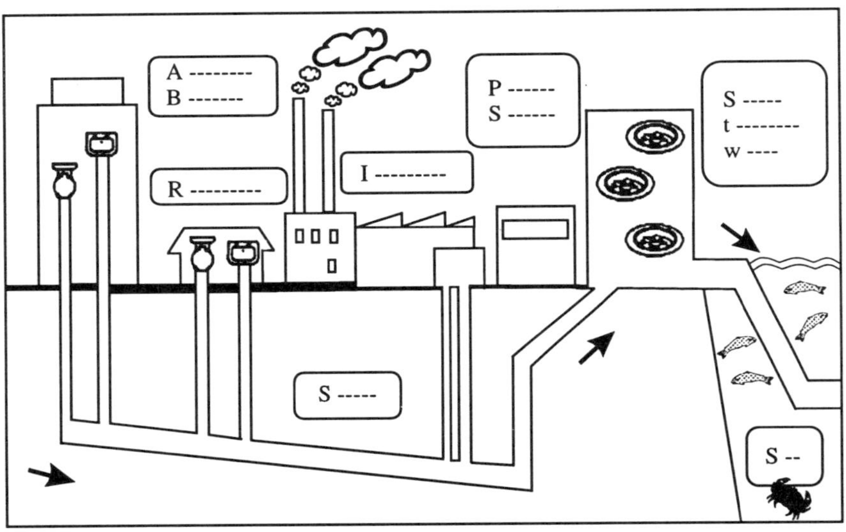

KEY

Symbol	Definition	Symbol	Definition
	toilet		smoke
	sink		treatment pool
	direction that waste water goes		

Activity Sheet #2—Disposal of Waste Water

The sewerage system is for the disposal of waste water.
The waste water in the sewers is pumped from the p______________ s______________ to the s______________ t______________ w______________.
The treated water is pumped out into the s__________.
Waste water from a______________, r______________, i______________ and other places goes into s______________.
At the s______________ t______________ works, the waste water is partially cleaned.
The sewers flow underground toward the pumping station.

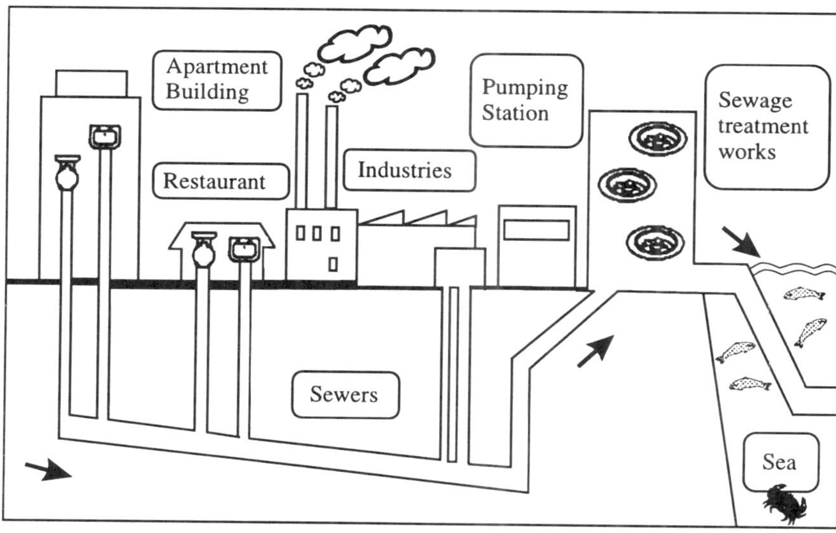

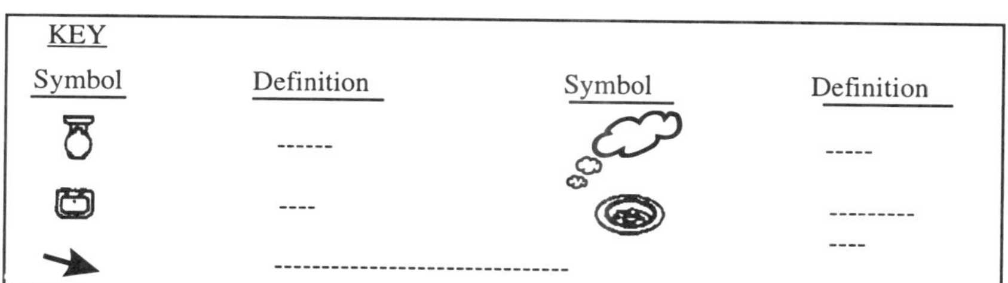

Activity Sheet #3—Disposal of Waste Water

The sewerage system is for the disposal of waste water.
The waste water in the sewers is pumped from the pumping station to the sewage treatment works.
The treated water is pumped out into the sea.
Waste water from apartments, restaurants, industries and other places goes into sewers.
At the sewage treatment works, the waste water is partially cleaned.
The sewers flow underground toward the pumping station.

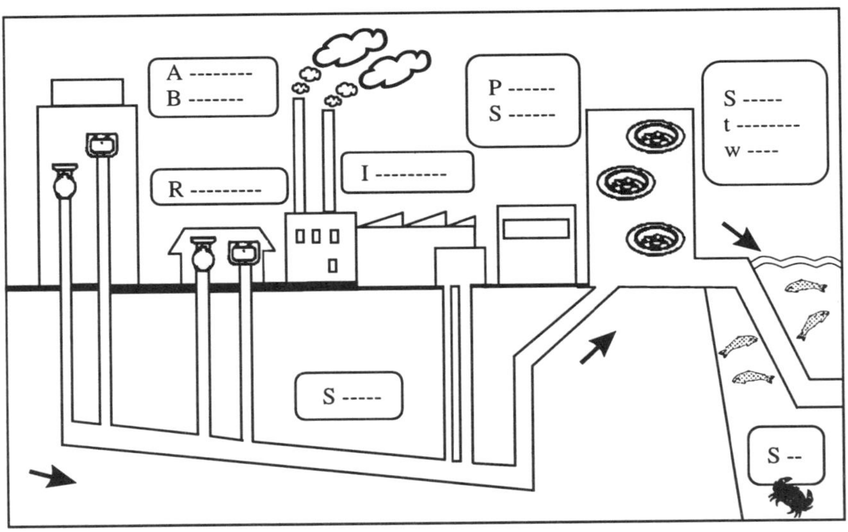

KEY

Symbol	Definition	Symbol	Definition
	------		-----
	----		--------- ----
	------------------------------		

Answer Key

The sewerage system is for the disposal of waste water.
The waste water in the sewers is pumped from the pumping station to the sewage treatment works.
The treated water is pumped out into the sea.
Waste water from apartments, restaurants, industries and other places goes into sewers.
The sewers flow underground toward the pumping station.
At the sewage treatment works, the waste water is partially cleaned.

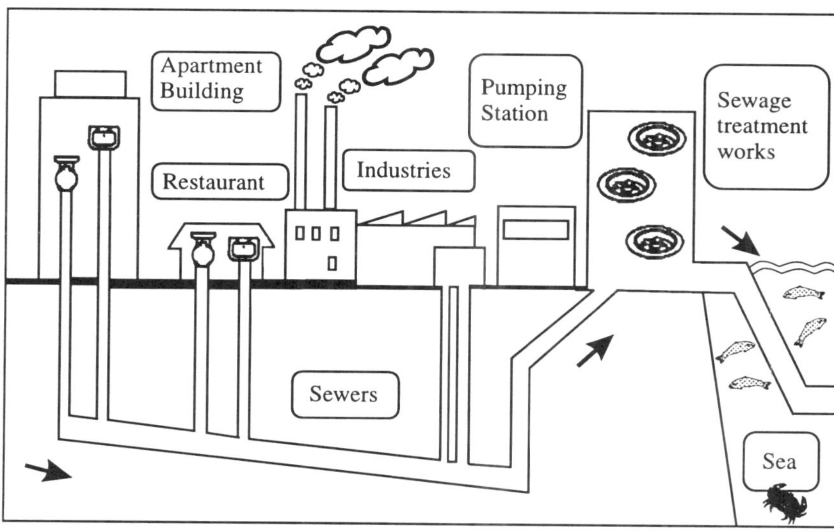

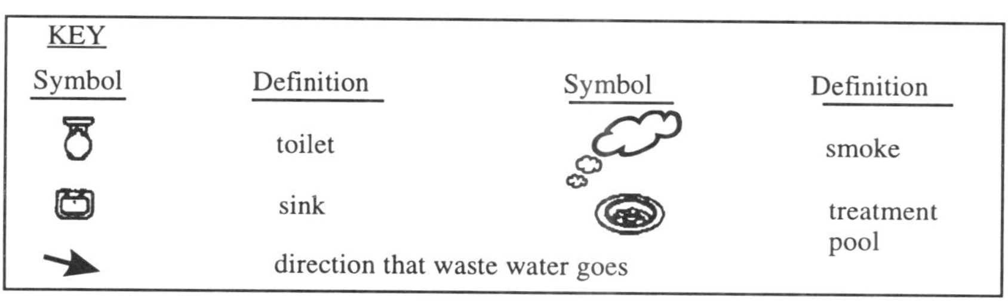

Haiku

INTRODUCTION

Haiku is a form of poetry with roots in ancient China and Japan. In the art and poetry of these cultures, nature is in the foreground. When humans are shown, they are usually small and in the background. Humans are part of the larger picture, in harmony with nature, not dominating it.

Haiku poets try to describe nature, its spirit and the feelings it inspires. Such an approach can heighten the writer's and reader's connection with nature. In the words of one poet, "Once one thinks like a mountain, the whole world is converted... one can also think like a black bear, becoming truly intimate with him... This is compassion, suffering with others."

Traditionally, haiku use three lines to create images that show how the poet feels or reacts to a specific event or scenario. The first line of a haiku has five syllables, the second has seven syllables, and the third has five syllables. The words do not usually rhyme.

ENVIRONMENTAL FOCUS

attitude

LANGUAGE FOCUS

finding alternative word choices, writing poetry, expressing feelings, describing nature

LANGUAGE SKILLS

writing

TIME

80 minutes

MATERIALS

three sample haiku written by Malaysian secondary school students and sent by Maygala Devi Ramadass, their teacher

Sample Haiku

Sun shining brightly
through the windows of my heart
—wonderful feeling.

Tomorrow will come
with the beautiful sunshine
and the damaged world.

Birds chirping loudly
wind singing a sweet song; please
save the earth—our home.

PREPARATION

Write the three sample haiku on the chalkboard or display them on a wall.

PROCEDURE

1. (*Whole class*) Teacher presents the background information on haiku and explains its technical elements.
2. (*Whole class*) Students read the haiku by the Malaysian students, discuss their possible meanings and look at how they fit the typical haiku structure.

Typical Haiku Structure

Line 1: 5 syllables
Line 2: 7 syllables
Line 3: 5 syllables.

3. (*Individual*) Each student writes one or more haiku. The teacher may wish to write some too. Teacher and students can bring in photos or visit natural sites in order to find inspiration.
4. (*Whole class*) Teacher coaches students in finding alternative word choices. See "Language Corner."
5. (*Pairs*) Students share their haiku with a partner. Partners react to the meaning of the new haiku. Students check their partner's haiku to see if they fit the structure. Teacher provides the following prompts for this discussion:

Prompt 1: Does it have the correct number of lines?

Prompt 2: Does it have the correct number of syllables per line?

Students make revisions based on feedback.

6. (*Whole class*) Students read their partner's haiku to the rest of the class.
7. (*Individual*) Students write their haiku on cardboard or poster board, illustrate them, then display them on the classroom walls.

VARIATIONS

1. Encourage students to visit particular sites, read articles about environmental issues or read other haiku. These things will give them ideas for their own creations.
2. Have students write haiku to accompany their notes or research in other subject areas. For example, they might include a haiku in a report on acid rain.

LANGUAGE CORNER: FINDING ALTERNATIVE WORD CHOICES

There are many sources, such as dictionaries and thesauruses, which students can use when searching for words for their haiku. Of course, care must be taken to be sure that a new word fits the context in which it is used. For this reason, it is a good practice to check the dictionary definitions of synonyms found in a thesaurus. The example below shows substitutes for "shining" and "damaged" found in the *Longman Language Activator Dictionary*. Students can look up some of the synonyms and discuss how appropriate each might be for the haiku in this lesson.

shining: glowing, gleaming, blazing, flashing, sparkling, twinkling, glittering, glowing in the dark

damaged: harmed, hurt, broken, vandalized, smashed up, sabotaged, tampered with, desecrated, defaced, worn away, corroded, eroded

Write Persuasive Letters!

INTRODUCTION

This activity gives students tools for taking action on environmental issues. One of the most favored actions by environmental activists is to write letters to well-known individuals and other people, companies, government bodies and organizations. This activity covers one possible format for a letter and envelope, plus one way to construct an argument.

ENVIRONMENTAL FOCUS

skills and participation—advocating actions to help the environment

LANGUAGE FOCUS

language for persuasion, format for writing a formal letter and addressing an envelope

LANGUAGE SKILLS

reading, writing

TIME

three 50-minute periods

MATERIALS

Blackline Master: Sample Letter
Blackline Master: Sample Envelope
Blackline Master: Letter Format
Blackline Master: Sample Envelope Format

PREPARATION

Make overheads of each of the blackline masters. Students can refer to these items during the discussion and while writing their letters.

PROCEDURE

1. (*Whole class*) Students read Blackline Master: Sample Letter and discuss what it means.

2. (*Whole class*) Teacher uses the sample letter to describe and illustrate the various features of a persuasive letter. These features include the following:

   - *Purpose:* To convince someone to consider a particular point of view or to take action regarding a specific concern.
   - *Language Features*: See "Language Corner."
   - *Text Organization*: Paragraph one introduces the issue or subject of the letter. Paragraph two provides the argument. Paragraph three makes recommendations. Paragraph four provides a summary and closing.

3. (*Whole class*) Students work together under the teacher's guidance to construct a persuasive letter. Bearing in mind the characteristics of a persuasive letter, the teacher or one of the students writes the letter as dictated by the class. To simplify the discussion, the letter should be written large enough for students to read. Write it on the chalkboard or an overhead transparency.
4. (*Groups*) Students form groups according to interests. They use Blackline Master: Letter Format as they work together to write group letters about an environmental issue that concerns them. Teacher provides feedback on the letters before they are sent.
5. (*Groups*) Students use Blackline Master: Sample Envelope and Blackline Master: Envelope Format to help them address their letters. They then mail them.
6. (*Groups*) If one or more letters receive a reply, groups analyze why the reply was written and consider what should be done in response to it.

VARIATIONS

1. For many countries, writing to local authorities and organizations may not involve English. Students can write these letters in the local language. They can use English to write to international organizations. Such organizations include the United Nations, the World Wildlife Fund (also known as WWF or World Wide Fund for Nature) and multinational corporations. Students can research the work of such organizations and their addresses.
2. After writing the letters outlined in this activity, students can write the reply they expect to receive. Students can exchange

their letters and compare them. If a reply comes to their letters, they can compare their expected replies with the real thing.

LANGUAGE CORNER: LANGUAGE FOR PERSUASION

People use specific words and structures to persuade others. Persuasive texts often include the following:

- *Emotional Adjectives*: These encourage the reader to react to the letter.
- *Causal Conjunctions*: Such conjunctions include *therefore, thus, in order to* and *as a result*. They tie the problem behavior to the unacceptable consequences.
- *Present Simple, Present Continuous and Present Perfect Tenses*: These tenses describe things that are happening now and things that have already happened and are still happening. They reinforce the idea that any past harm has present consequences.
- *Passive Voice*: This makes the action on the object more important than who or what is doing it.
- *Imperative*: This orders or encourages the recipient to do something about the issue.
- *Generalizations*: These are often effective in showing the widespread effect of an action.

Have students look for examples of each of the above devices as they read the sample letter. Encourage them to use most of these devices in their own letters.

Sample Letter

Mohamed Yusof
8 Jalan Kebun
Kota Indah
Selangor
Malaysia

20th March 1998

Mr. P. Rajendran
Ministry of the Environment
Jalan Bumidaya
Kuala Lumpur
Malaysia

Dear Mr. Rajendran,

We are students from Meranti High School in Kota Indah. We are writing to you to voice our concern about the terrible pollution caused by the number of cars we have in our city.

When we were little children, we used to dream about our city as a clean place with lots of fresh air and green trees. Now that we are older, we realize that our dream is impossible because the trees have been cut down to build roads and the roads are so crowded with cars that the air is full of pollution. Every day, more and more people move to the city looking for jobs. Public transport cannot cater to such a large number of people. As a result, many people drive cars.

We would like to make three suggestions for reducing pollution. First, please provide more public transport so that fewer people need to drive cars. Second, in order to raise money for public transport, increase the price of petrol for private cars. This will discourage people from driving. Therefore, more of them will use public transport. Finally, please encourage companies and government offices to move away from the city. As a result, the city will become less crowded and therefore less polluted.

Thank you for considering our suggestions. We look forward to receiving your reply.

Yours faithfully,

Mohamed Yusof
Class Monitor on behalf of Class 4H

Sample Envelope

M. Yusof
8 Jalan Kebun
Kota Indah
Selangor
Malaysia

Mr P. Rajendran
Ministry of Environment
Jalan Bumidaya
Kuala Lumpur
Malaysia

Letter Format

Writer's name
Writer's address

Date

Receiver's name
Receiver's address

Greeting (e.g., Dear Mr. Chan, Dear Madam or Dear Sir),

The first paragraph provides the subject and purpose of the letter. This introduces the issue to be discussed.

The second paragraph provides arguments on the issue.

The third paragraph makes recommendations for solving the problem.

The final paragraph provides a summary of what was discussed and a complimentary closing.

Formal closing (e.g., Yours sincerely, Yours faithfully or Cordially yours),

Signature of writer
Title of writer

Envelope Format

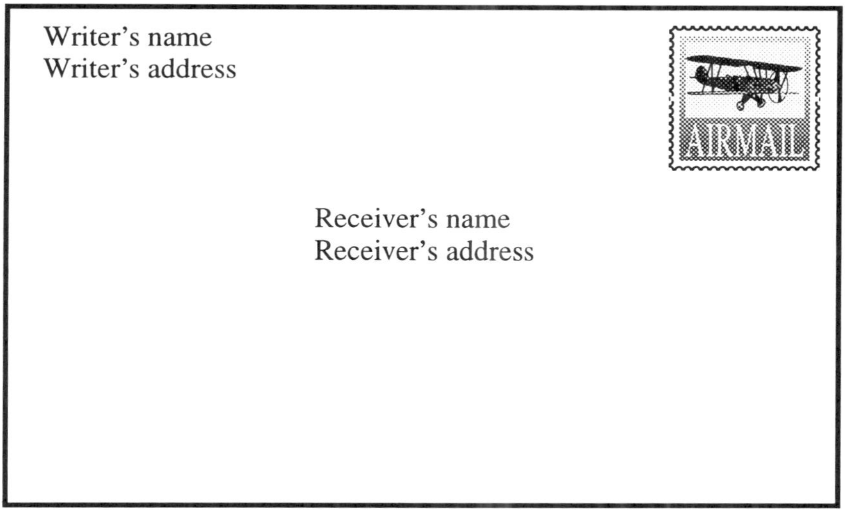

Analyze Data about the Environment

INTRODUCTION

This lesson provides opportunities for students to discuss the relative roles of industrialized countries and those that are less industrialized. It also involves the question of sustainable development and provides scope for teaching language across the curriculum.

The data demonstrate a striking phenomenon. Industrialized countries such as the United States are much wealthier and use many more resources than do less industrialized countries such as Brazil and India. This is evident when the following three statistics are compared:

- *Gross Domestic Product per Capita*: This refers to the value of domestic output per person. It is a broad indicator of the wealth a country produces.
- Carbon Emissions from Fossil Fuels per Capita: This refers to the estimated number of tons of carbon dioxide per capita added to the air from burning fossil fuels for such purposes as driving cars, running factories and heating or cooling indoor air. Because carbon dioxide is one of the main forms of air pollution and is believed to contribute to global warming, such data provide an indicator of how much a country contributes to polluting the earth's atmosphere.
- *Life Expectancy*: This is influenced by many factors, such as access to food, medical care and clean water. A great deal of environmentally-unfriendly construction is necessary to secure safe water for people. On the other hand, unsafe drinking water is a major environmental hazard for poor people, contributing to millions of deaths every year.

ENVIRONMENTAL FOCUS

understanding and evaluative ability—the role of wealth and poverty in the environmental crisis

LANGUAGE FOCUS

reading tables and figures, forming comparatives and superlatives

LANGUAGE SKILLS

speaking, reading tables and figures, encouraging others to participate

TIME

50 minutes

MATERIALS

Blackline Master: Gross Domestic Product per Capita (US dollars)
Blackline Master: Carbon Emissions from Fossil Fuels per Capita (tons)
Blackline Master: GDP Compared to Carbon Emissions and Life Expectancy
Blackline Master: Life Expectancy (years)
Blackline Master: Comprehension Questions
Blackline Master: Discussion Questions

Answer Key for Comprehension Questions

Suggested Answers for Discussion Questions

Answer Key for Comprehension Questions

1. (a) USA
   (b) India
2. (a) USA
   (b) India
3. Cars, factories
4. Carbon emissions cause air pollution and contribute to global warming.
5. (a) USA
   (b) India
6. Many of the factors that contribute to a longer life, such as clean water and adequate food, potentially harm the environment. For example, to have clean water, countries need to spend a lot of money to clean the water and build systems of pipes to carry it. On the other hand, protecting the environment helps people live longer lives. For instance, polluted water is a major cause of disease and death in poor countries. Every year, millions of people die from diseases caused by unclean water.

7. It takes about 13 Brazilians or about 17 Indians to equal the carbon emissions from fossil fuels of one person in the United States.

Suggested Answers for Discussion Questions

1. They could use less by choosing techniques that use fewer natural resources. Bicycling instead of driving is one such technique. They might also invent ways of keeping their lifestyle but using fewer resources. For example, they might develop a vehicle that runs on non-fossil fuel.
2. We could use the following methods to convince people in industrialized countries to conserve resources:
   - help them to understand that we are all on the same planet and need to consider everyone's needs;
   - ask them to consider how their actions will affect future generations;
   - point out the advantages of reduced resource consumption;
   - encourage governments to impose taxes on resource consumption;
   - provide tax advantages for resource conservation; and
   - encourage conserving lifestyles.
3. Some people in less industrialized countries need to use more resources just to survive. There are several ways to raise standards of living without doing as much harm to the environment as industrialized countries are now doing:
   - Countries might develop alternative sources of energy. For example, Brazil makes ethanol fuel from sugar cane. Ethanol replaces gasoline in many vehicles and for some industrial uses.
   - Individuals might promote and practice alternative lifestyles that use fewer resources.
   - Individuals can encourage governments and corporations to do their share by voting for parties concerned about the environment and buying goods from companies with environmental programs.
4. Only if it is done in an efficient way that considers the environment.
5. There are differences in wealth, technological innovation, power and lifestyle.

6. Yes, there are large differences. Some wealthy people in less industrialized countries use as much as or more than the average person in industrialized countries. Some poor people in industrialized countries, as well as those who are concerned about the environment, use much less than the average.

PREPARATION

Prepare copies of the blackline masters that provide data for each student or group of students.
Prepare overhead transparencies of Blackline Master: Comprehension Questions and Blackline Master: Discussion Questions.

PROCEDURE

1. (*Whole class*) Teacher introduces and explains the following terms: gross domestic product, carbon emissions from fossil fuels per capita and life expectancy. Teacher has students look at and discuss the information on the table and bar graphs.
2. (*Pairs*) Students form pairs, making sure that at least one person in the pair is strong in mathematics. Pairs do the comprehension questions, with one person trying the odd-numbered questions and the other the even-numbered questions. They check each other's work.
3. (*Whole class*) Teacher asks for answers from pairs and also for an explanation of how the answers were obtained.
4. (*Groups*) In groups of four, students discuss the implications of using the data to deal with the environmental crisis. While discussing, individual students take on one of the following roles: recorder, encourager, timekeeper and reporter. For more information about these roles, see "Group Roles" in the opening section.

VARIATIONS

1. Students research an environmental problem and display their data using charts and graphs. Students keep the class posted on any improvements or deterioration in the situation.
2. Students choose a subject such as population increase, the rate of deforestation or the number of endangered animals remaining. Students research the relevant data, then make a

chart or graph from reused materials such as paper, cardboard, drinking straws and other household items.

3. Students work with the mathematics teachers to do other mathematical and graphical applications using the data in this activity.

LANGUAGE CORNER: COMPARATIVES AND SUPERLATIVES

It is useful for students to learn to use comparatives and superlatives to help them discuss data. This language corner presents four different structures for forming comparatives and superlatives.

Adjectives with One Syllable

Comparative Structure: adjective + *-er* + *than*
Comparative Example: high = *higher than*

Superlative Structure: *the* + adjective + *-est*
Superlative Example: low = *the lowest*

Adjectives Ending in a Single Consonant after a Vowel

Comparative Structure: Double the consonant before adding *-er* + *than*
Comparative Example: fat = *fatter than*

Superlative Structure: *the* + Double the consonant before adding *-est*
Superlative Example: big = *the biggest*

Adjectives with Two or More Syllables Plus Some Irregular Adjectives

Comparative Structure: *less* or *more* + adjective + *than*
Comparative Example: generous = *less generous than*
wasteful = *more wasteful than*

Superlative Structure: *the* + *least* or *most* + adjective
Superlative Example: toxic = *the least toxic*
harmful = *the most harmful*

Two-syllable Adjectives Ending in -y with a Consonant before the -y

Comparative Structure: Drop the *-y* and add *-ier* + *than*
Comparative Example: dirty = *dirtier than*

Superlative Structure: *the* + Drop the *-y* and add *-iest*
Superlative Example: easy = *the easiest*

Gross Domestic Product per Capita (US dollars)

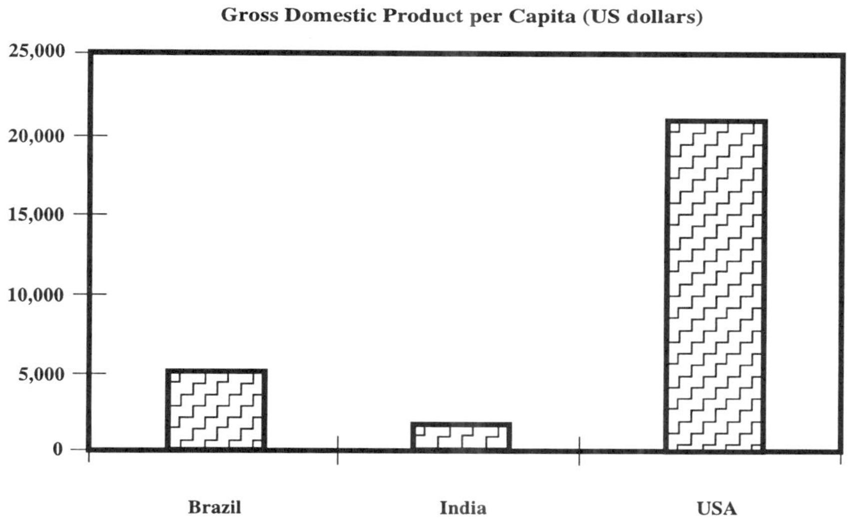

Carbon Emissions from Fossil Fuels per Capita (tons)

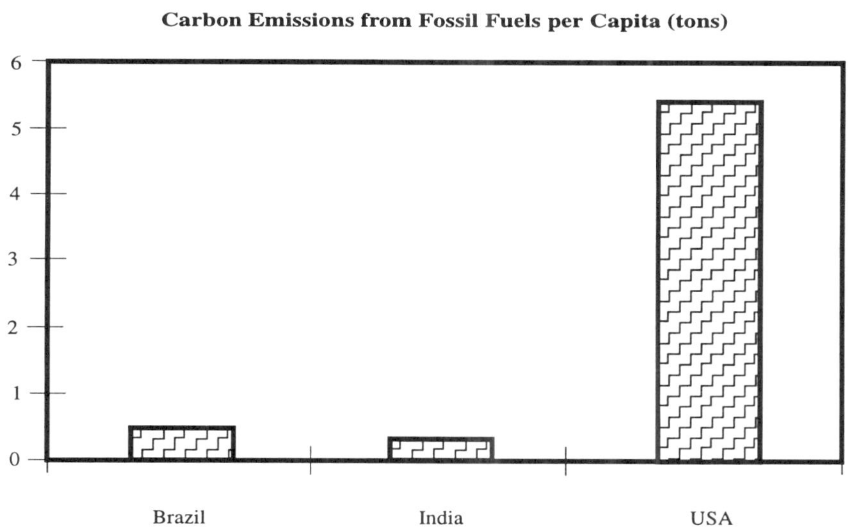

GDP Compared to Carbon Emissions and Life Expectancy

Countries	*Gross Domestic Product per Capita (US dollars)*	*Carbon Emissions per Capita (tons)*	*Life Expectancy (years)*
Brazil	5 000	0.4	62
India	1 300	0.3	59
USA	21 800	5.3	76

Life Expectancy (years)

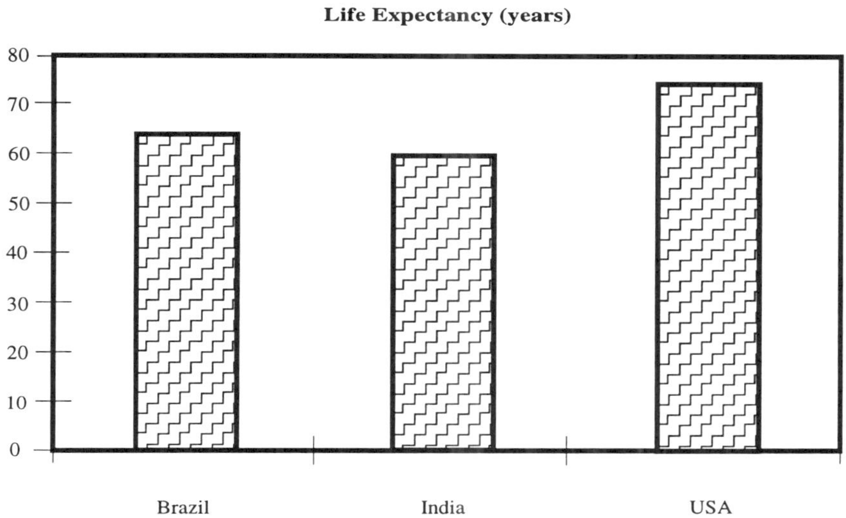

Comprehension Questions

Use the information on the four data sheets to answer the following questions. Before starting, review the meaning of the terms below.

• *Gross Domestic Product (GDP) per Capita*
This is the average amount that a person in the country produces in one year. For example, if the GDP is $5 000, the average person produces $5 000 worth of goods in one year. The term, *per capita* means "per person." It is calculated by dividing the total amount of product produced by the country by the number of people in the country.

• *Carbon Emissions from Fossil Fuels per Capita*
This is a measure of how much fossil fuel the country burns in one year. To get "per capita" data, that amount is divided by the number of people in the country.

When fossil fuels are burned, carbon is emitted. For instance, carbon is released by cars burning gasoline or petrol and factories burning oil. Countries with high carbon emissions per capita are doing a lot of harm to the Earth's environment.

• *Life Expectancy*
This refers to the average number of years a person in the country usually lives. On the average, females have a slightly higher life expectancy than males.

1. (a) Which country has the highest per capita GDP?
   (b) Which has the lowest?

2. (a) Which country produces the largest amount of carbon emissions per person?
   (b) Which produces the lowest?

3. What are some of the main sources of carbon emissions?

4. How do carbon emissions affect the environment?

5. (a) Which country has the highest life expectancy?
   (b) Which has the lowest?

6. How is life expectancy connected to the environment?

7. Brazil and India are less industrialized than the United States. How many people from each of Brazil and India does it take to equal the carbon emissions from fossil fuels per capita in the United States?

   HINT : To get the answer, divide the per capita figure for the United States by the per capita figures for each of Brazil and India. Show the result with drawings. For example, use a drawing of one person from the United States beside the number of people from Brazil that it takes to equal that one person's amount of carbon emissions. If the United States had five times the amount of carbon emissions of Brazil, you would place one figure beside the United States and five beside Brazil.

Discussion Questions

In a group, discuss the questions below. Remember to encourage each other to provide ideas and responses for each question.

1. How might people in industrialized countries such as the United States use fewer resources?

2. How could you try to convince people in such countries to use less?

3. Should people in less industrialized countries use more?

4. Can people in less industrialized countries have more of the things that people in industrialized countries have without doing more harm to the environment?

5. Why is there such a big gap between the industrialized and less industrialized countries?

6. Do you think that everyone in the countries on the chart has the same lifestyle or are there differences, small or large, between people in the same country? For example, does everyone in the United States cause the same amount of carbon emissions from fossil fuels?

Experiment With Mind Maps

INTRODUCTION

Creating mind maps (also known as semantic maps, word webs and spider maps) gives students a non-linear tool for organizing information and seeing the connections between ideas. Mapping is useful in reading comprehension, vocabulary development and pre-writing. The interconnected nature of the environment makes it a great topic to use with mapping. The completed mind map, when displayed, can help to educate other members of the school and community.

ENVIRONMENTAL FOCUS

knowledge—overcoming various environmental dangers

LANGUAGE FOCUS

organizing information into mind maps

SKILLS

speaking, reading, writing

TIME

approximately 2 hours

MATERIALS

Teacher Script: Animal Trade
Blackline Master: Sample Mind Map
Blackline Master: Text #1—Overcoming Water Pollution
Blackline Master: Text #2—Conserving Energy
Blackline Master: Text #3—Reversing Deforestation
Blackline Master: Text #4—Improving Air Quality

Teacher Script: Animal Trade

The title of this mind map is "animal trade." "Animal trade" is written in large, bold, capital letters.

This sample mind map provides three reasons for people trading animals: for food, parts and experiments. These three words are also printed in bold, capital letters. They are connected to "animal trade" by link lines. These link lines show a relationship between the ideas.

"Food," "parts" and "experiments" are first-level ideas. They are linked to "Animal trade" to show that animals are traded for those three reasons.

Let's think further about each of the reasons for animal trade. For example, what animal parts are traded?

Both ivory and rhinoceros horn are traded. These are referred to as second-level ideas. They are connected to the first-level ideas to which they are related. In this case, they are connected to "parts." Note that second-level ideas are capitalized.

When you consider how trade in ivory has affected elephant populations, you may decide that this trade should be banned. This is a third-level idea. It is connected to ivory and rhinoceros horn because it is related to both of these ideas.

Notice the arrows connecting "Whales" to "Ban trade." Whales are hunted for food. Hunting whales has also affected whale populations. Perhaps whale hunting should be banned too. The arrows linking "Whales" and "Ban trade" are called cross-link lines because they link ideas in different sections of the mind map.

Let's look at another example.

Animals are also traded for experiments. One example of this is "Monkeys for AIDS research." This is a second-level idea.

Are there alternatives to this trade? Yes, similar information might be available by developing computer simulations. That's why "Computer simulation" is printed as a third-level idea.

There are no cross-link lines between computer simulation and rhino horn because we aren't yet aware of a computer simulation for this substance. On the other hand, we could cross-link "Ban trade" and "Monkeys for AIDS research."

PREPARATION

Put the sample mind map on an overhead transparency or reproduce it to display on the classroom walls or chalkboard.

Make one set of the four blackline master texts for each group of four students.

PROCEDURE

1. *(Groups)* Students form home teams consisting of four people. (See "Jigsaw" in the opening section.)

2. (*Whole class*) Teacher displays and explains the sample mind map.
3. (*Group*) Each home team member receives a different text related to the topic. Group members leave their home teams and form expert teams with two or three others who have the same text. The expert team's task is to work together to create a mind map which will later be used to teach their text to the other members of their home team. Once the team has completed its mind map, team members each make a copy for themselves.
4. (*Group*) Home teams reassemble. One at a time, the members use their mind maps to teach their team members about their particular topic. Some members may modify their mind maps based on questions and suggestions from their home team members.
5. (*Groups*) After everyone has taken a turn teaching, the home team works together to create one big map or chart showing different ways the environment is damaged and how it can be protected. Team members look for ways that they can create cross-links between the four different topics.
6. (*Whole class*) Students post their mind maps on classroom, school or community center walls.

VARIATIONS

1. Mind maps are very useful tools for pre-writing. Students can use mind maps to organize their writing. Other members of the class who have helped to create the mind maps can provide feedback about the writing.
2. Students can make more dynamic mind maps by using different kinds of materials. For example, disc shapes cut out of cardboard can be used to form sections of a map. This method is particularly useful for changing mind maps. As more information is added, discs can be moved and replaced without completely redrawing the map.

LANGUAGE CORNER

Mind maps are a distinct language tool. They assist students with writing, note-taking and other similar tasks. They are also useful for generating ideas and vocabulary, as well as helping students to organize their ideas prior to writing.

Students can start by writing their topic in the middle of a blank page. They then brainstorm related ideas and write these around the main topic. These are the first-level ideas. Next, students consider ideas related to the first-level ideas. These are second-level ideas. Students write these ideas around the outside of the mind map.

Students can draw lines that connect ideas in different parts of the mind map. These are called link lines. They should be labeled to show the relationship between the connected ideas.

Students should work in pencil. They may want to erase and move certain ideas as they consider new ways to connect them.

Once they have completed the mind map, students can consider which ideas are appropriate to the particular audience or purpose they wish to address. They can then use each second-level idea as the subject of a paragraph. First-level ideas provide section headings for the paper.

Sample Mind Map

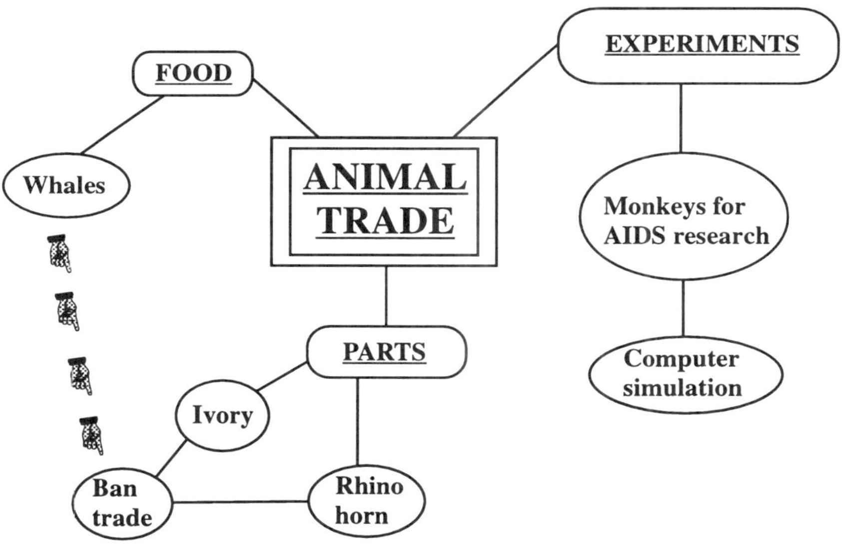

Text #1—Overcoming Water Pollution

People are responsible for polluting the water in lakes, rivers and oceans, as well as under the ground. Water pollution means that there is less clean water for people and land animals. There is less water for drinking and for recreation. In addition, there are fewer places for water animals to live.

There are many sources of water pollution, including sewage, industrial waste, oil spills and deforestation. Each of these sources is discussed below. There are also suggestions for possible solutions to each type of pollution.

Sewage comes from both homes and industries. Home owners, business people and the government can work together to lessen this source of pollution. We can avoid pouring harmful substances into sinks and toilets. Also, we could buy products which do not harm the environment. Governments can set up sewage treatment plants. These plants filter household sewage before it is released into bodies of water. Industrial sewage often contains poisonous chemicals. Industries could treat their own sewage.

Oil is carried all over the world in ships. It has many uses. Oil is used to fuel cars and to generate electricity. Sometimes the ships carrying oil leak. As a result, oil spills into the ocean. This pollutes the water and kills plants and animals. There are at least three ways to lessen this risk of pollution. We can use less oil. We can develop alternatives to oil use such as building cars that run on solar energy, or energy from the sun. We can insist that all oil tankers have double hulls. This will reduce the chances of oil leaking into the ocean.

Trees often grow along river banks and seashores. Their roots help to hold the soil in place. If trees are cut down, heavy rain can wash soil into rivers and seas. This is a problem for several reasons. Too much soil in the water can cover the places where fish lay their eggs, thus preventing reproduction. Soil can also carry pollution from homes and industries. Soil pollution can be prevented by banning logging in shore areas and by replanting trees in places where they have been removed.

Although solving the problem of water pollution is not easy, it is possible. Progress has already been made in many areas of the world. Some rivers which were once heavy with pollution are now clean and usable. It is up to us to help clean up other polluted bodies of water and rivers.

Text #2—Conserving Energy

Energy is so much a part of our daily lives that we often take it for granted. For example, we use energy from gas, electricity and wood to cook. We use energy from petrol/gasoline and motor oil to travel. We also use energy to run entertaining machines such as televisions and stereos. Unfortunately, much of the energy we use comes from fossil fuels such as oil and coal. As a result, our energy use contributes to the destruction of our environment. Fortunately, there are many solutions to this problem. These include reducing energy use and using alternative energy sources.

A lot of energy is used in buildings and in transportation. There are many ways we can reduce the amount of energy used in these two areas. In buildings, we can lower the amount of heating or air-conditioning we use. We can also make sure that lights and appliances are switched off when not in use. When shopping, we can buy electrical equipment that uses less energy. For example, some computers, ovens and washing machines have power-saving features.

Ways to reduce the amount of energy used in transportation include walking or riding a bicycle. Another idea is to take public transport such as buses or trains. If we have to use private cars, we can try to share with other people so that there are fewer cars on the road.

Using energy from sources other than fossil fuels is another way of protecting the environment. Sources of alternative energy include solar, wind and wave power. Solar energy has been used to heat water and houses. Wind and wave power have been harnessed to generate electricity. Support from individuals, governments and corporations is necessary if we want to increase use of alternative sources of energy.

Many people around the world are becoming richer. Once they have enough money, many are eager to buy the convenience and pleasure that comes from products which use energy. We need to remember to use energy wisely in order to ensure that this convenience and pleasure is not at the expense of our environment. After all, we have only one planet!

Text #3—Reversing Deforestation

Forests safeguard the health of our planet. They protect the soil, provide water, regulate the climate and provide a home for thousands of animal and plant species. Unfortunately, forests are being cut down all over the world, both for timber and to provide land for agriculture and development. Possible solutions for the problems of deforestation are presented below.

Extensive logging of forests can cause soil erosion, extensive flooding and the extinction of many animals and plants. To prevent this damage, governments must take steps immediately. Forests can be turned into national parks which will promote tourism in the country. In this way, stopping logging can actually generate money for the national economy. Governments also need to pass laws to control logging. They can make sure that these laws are strictly enforced and punish any illegal loggers.

Another idea is to plant trees. A "Go-Green" campaign can be organized to encourage individuals, schools and offices to plant more trees in cities and along roads. Trees should also be planted in areas where they have already been cut down. In order to prevent soil erosion and flooding, logged areas should be replanted immediately after the trees have been cut down. Reforestation, unfortunately, cannot save the many plants and animals that are lost when the original trees are removed. Therefore, forest areas that are especially rich in animal and plant species should be preserved as national parks.

Another way to save trees is to find ways to grow food and to house people which do not require destroying forests. Hydroponic farming is one such method. Using this technique, fruit and vegetables are grown in water instead of soil. To reduce the amount of materials needed for housing, developers can build high-rise buildings instead of single- or double-storey houses and bungalows. This will reduce the pressure for more land.

We should all be concerned about saving the forests. Trees are beautiful and useful. They have a right to grow tall and strong and to live a long life! In addition, trees purify the air that we breathe. If we do not act quickly to save them, we are actually contributing to our own destruction!

Text #4—Improving Air Quality

The air that we breathe is not safe anymore. For more than a century, it has been polluted by poisons coming from factories, motor vehicles and power stations. The number and severity of respiratory or breathing diseases are increasing. How can we help to reduce this problem? There are many ways.

Factories emit many different kinds of poisonous gases and fumes which pollute the air. To reduce pollution, factories can use pollution-control filters in their smoke stacks. They can also change their manufacturing processes so that they give off less poisonous gases. Governments should be involved in taking action against factories that are releasing excessive fumes and gases. Governments can also encourage the development of technology that removes many pollutants so that they are not released to the environment.

The number of motor vehicles on the road is increasing at a frightening rate. This not only causes traffic congestion but also increases air pollution. One way we can reduce this problem is by organizing car pools. Other ideas include using public transport, walking or riding a bicycle. Using unleaded petrol can also help.

Humans cannot live for more than a few minutes without air. Thus, clean air is a precious but rapidly disappearing resource. Many countries have realized the serious dangers of air pollution and have taken steps to reduce it. Success depends on each and every individual playing a part in keeping the air free of pollution. Only then can we all breathe a sigh of relief.

Communicate Your Point of View

INTRODUCTION

Language is not objective. It is often used subjectively to help people achieve their ends. This is reflected in the way that people with different viewpoints write about the same topic. When students can identify the various techniques that writers use to convince readers to accept their point of view about an issue, they can begin to use some of these techniques in their own writing. This will enable them to read and write more effectively.

ENVIRONMENTAL FOCUS

skills and evaluative ability—controversial issues

LANGUAGE FOCUS

passive and active voice, using grammar, content and vocabulary to assist in expressing a particular viewpoint

SKILLS

reading, writing

TIME

50 minutes over two days

MATERIALS

Blackline Master: Seal Hunt #1
Blackline Master: Seal Hunt #2
Text Comparison

Text Comparison

	Seal Hunt #1	*Seal Hunt #2*
Grammar	uses active voice, which makes it clear who does the killing	uses passive voice, which does not mention who does the killing
Content	mentions that the seals are babies	suggests that average people use seal products
Word Choice	uses harsh words such as brutally, violently and cruel to describe the hunt uses endearing words such as innocent and beautiful to describe the seals	uses nice words such as painlessly, quality, scientific, beautiful and enjoy to describe the hunt and its results

PREPARATION

Make one copy of each blackline master for each pair of students.

PROCEDURE

1. (*Whole class*) Teacher provides any necessary background on the hunting of seals.

   Teacher: Every year, baby seals are killed for their fur. This is usually done by clubbing them to death. The killing is done soon after the young seal's birth when it is lying helpless on the ice. Many people are opposed to this killing. Others point out that seal hunting is a business that provides jobs. It is no worse than killing lambs or calves for food.

2. (*Individual*) Students read Seal Hunt #1 and Seal Hunt #2. Students underline words that show the writers' attitudes toward what is happening.

3. (*Whole class*) Teacher leads students in a comparison of the two texts using ideas such as those outlined in "Text Comparison."
4. *(Individual)* Students find texts about issues, including local ones, and analyze them, looking at how language is used to express the author's viewpoint. Environmental groups, embassies and corporations can be good sources for such texts.
5. *(Pairs)* In pairs, students choose a controversial environmental issue that interests them. One member of the pair writes a text supporting one point of view on that issue. The other member writes supporting an opposing point of view on the same issue. They exchange papers and look for the devices discussed in #3.

VARIATIONS

1. Teacher finds two texts about the same subject but with different viewpoints, then cuts sentences or groups of sentences into strips. Students study the language in the sentences and decide which sentences belong to which text. In the process, they pay attention to writing style and how it affects what is written.
2. Students write a class newsletter in which different opinions are given about current environmental issues.

LANGUAGE CORNER: PASSIVE VOICE

The passive voice was first discussed in "Understanding Diagrams." The language corner in that activity explained why people use the passive voice. This language corner explains various ways to form the passive. Generally, the passive is formed using the verb *to be* and the past participle of the verb.

Present Tense

Structure: correct form of present tense of *to be* + past participle of verb

Example: I *am impressed* by that work.
She *is hurt* by your comment.
Trees *are planted.*

Past Tense

Structure: correct form of past tense of *to be* + past participle of verb

Example:	He *was hit* by the car. Trees *were removed.*

Future Tense

Structure#1:	correct form of future tense of *to be* + past participle of verb
Example:	Trees *will be shredded.*
Structure #2:	correct form of present tense of *to be* + *going to be* + past participle of verb
Example:	I *am going to be attacked.* Baby seals *are going to be killed.*

Seal Hunt #1

Every year, profit-hungry companies murder hundreds of thousands of baby seals. They kill these innocent animals by brutally clubbing them to death. They then violently rip their skins off their bodies in order to make needless luxury products. In the end, a few people get rich from the cruel, senseless slaying of these beautiful animals.

Seal Hunt #2

Every year, hundreds of thousands of consumers buy seal products. In order to provide quality seal skins for these products, seals are harvested as quickly and painlessly as possible. Scientific methods are used to ensure that the process is a humane one. The seal skins are then removed and tanned using the most modern techniques. The result is beautiful products enjoyed by people around the world.

Rights and Responsibilities

INTRODUCTION

The idea of human rights is well known. Nature should have rights too. This activity begins with students thinking about the rights of children, then extends the vision of rights to include nature. Students' empathy for nature may increase as they take on the roles of various parts of the environment.

ENVIRONMENTAL FOCUS

attitude—the rights of nature

LANGUAGE FOCUS

modals

LANGUAGE SKILLS

writing, speaking

TIME

Part 1: 40 minutes
Part 2: 30 minutes
Part 3: two periods of 40 minutes each

MATERIALS

Blackline Master: UN Declaration of the Rights of the Child (please see page 99)

PREPARATION

Either place the UN Declaration of the Rights of the Child on an overhead or ask some students to make a big poster displaying it.

PROCEDURE

Part 1

1. (*Individual*) Students work alone to make a list of what rights they think children should have.
2. (*Pairs*) Students form pairs, discuss their lists and compile them so that they have only one list between them.

3. (*Whole class*) Pairs of students share their lists with the class. Students then work together to attempt to categorize the items on the various lists.

Sample Categories

- right to get enough food
- right to have enough nutrition
- right to learn to read and write
- right to learn about the world

The first two items can be combined into a nutrition category. The last two can be combined into an education category.

4. (*Individual*) Students select one category which they personally feel is important. They write a report on this topic.

Part 2

1. *(Whole class)* Teacher displays the UN Declaration of the Rights of the Child.

Teacher: This was ratified by the member countries of the United Nations. The rights are not necessarily listed in order of importance. They all explain something which every child has a right to have.

Students discuss each right, what it means and whether or not they receive any benefit from this right.

2. *(Groups)* Students form groups of four with different partners than in Part 1 and discuss any changes they would make to the UN list. They then rank the rights on the UN list in order of importance. To facilitate discussion, students can take turns explaining which right they would rank as first, second, third, etc.
3. *(Whole class)* Groups report the results of their discussions to the class.

Part 3

1. *(Whole class)* Students briefly discuss the concept of rights for nature.
2. *(Groups)* Students divide into the same groups used in Part 2. These are the students' home teams. (See "Jigsaw" in the opening section.) In their home teams, students choose to represent one of the following aspects of nature: plants, humans, other land animals or water animals.

3. *(Groups)* Students leave their home teams and form expert groups with others who represent the same part of nature. These groups discuss the rights of their part of nature and list them using the structures explained in "Language Corner."
4. *(Groups)* Students reassemble into their home teams. Individual members share what they discussed in their expert groups and use that information to help their group develop a list of the rights of nature. Groups write up and display their lists.
5. *(Whole class)* Students discuss the lists, consider examples of where the rights of nature are being violated and decide what they can do to help protect these rights.

VARIATIONS

1. Students can illustrate the rights of nature by producing posters with illustrations and captions that highlight each right.
2. Students can develop a list of ways that humans are responsible for the protection of nature's rights.

LANGUAGE CORNER: MODALS AND PHRASAL MODALS OF NECESSITY

In English, there are many ways to show necessity. This language corner deals with the use of *must*, which is a modal, and the use of *have to* and *have got to*, which are phrasal modals.

Structure 1: Must is a modal. Modals do not change form to agree with the subject.
Example: Plants *must* have a place to grow.
A land animal *must* be able to breathe clean air.

Structure 2: *Have to* and *have got to* are phrasal modals. Phrasal modals do change to agree with the subject. Only the verb part of the phrasal modal changes.
Example: Humans think that they *have to* have modern conveniences, such as cars.
A water animal *has got to* have enough oxygen to breathe.

This activity was adapted from "Child rights—Earth rights" by A. Greene (*Green Teacher*, Volume 33 (1993.) *Green Teacher* can be contacted at 95 Robert Street, Toronto, Ontario, M5S 2K5 Canada.

UN Declaration of the Rights of the Child

- The right to affection, love and understanding.
- The right to adequate nutrition and medical care.
- The right to free education.
- The right to full opportunity for play and recreation.
- The right to a name and nationality.
- The right to special care if handicapped.
- The right to be among the first to receive relief in times of disaster.
- The right to be a useful member of society and to develop individual abilities.
- The right to be brought up in a spirit of peace and universal brotherhood.
- The right to enjoy these rights regardless of race, color, sex, religion or national or social origin.

Cooperative Controversies

INTRODUCTION

When used constructively, controversies can facilitate student learning. They motivate students, help them see different perspectives and provide opportunities for practice in the four skills. Discussing controversies helps students to build cooperative skills needed to promote team work and aids in the forming of opinions. The environment provides many opportunities to discuss controversies. Should a particular forest be cut down? Is it right to use violent methods to protect the environment? Should medical experiments be done on animals? The cooperative controversy technique outlined here is one way of encouraging students to think about these and other important issues while they are developing their language and reasoning abilities. The following activity gives an example of how the technique works. Although it concentrates on a discussion about whether humans should kill animals for food, any debatable topic related to the environment could be used.

ENVIRONMENTAL FOCUS

evaluative ability—controversial environmental issues

LANGUAGE FOCUS

non-verbal communication

SKILLS

speaking

TIME

two 40-minute periods

PROCEDURE

1. (*Groups*) Students form groups of four. Each foursome divides into two pairs. Each pair is assigned one position. One pair supports the idea of people using animals for food. The other pair opposes the use of animals for food. Each pair prepares a series of arguments to support their side.

2. (*Groups*) Pairs present their positions on the controversy to their foursome, with each member taking an equal part in the presentation.
3. (*Groups*) After both sides present their ideas, the group of four students discusses the issue back and forth, trying to convince the other pair that their assigned point of view is the best one. (See "Language Corner.")
4. (*Groups*) Pairs change positions and prepare a presentation on the opposite viewpoint. Those who were against killing animals now argue for killing. Those who were for the use of animals for food now oppose the idea. Students prepare a new set of arguments, then repeat steps #2 and #3 with their new positions.
5. (*Groups*) Students are no longer assigned positions. They are free to choose their own point of view. The group discusses the issue and tries to reach a consensus. (Don't worry if students don't reach consensus. It is the discussion and consideration of different points of view that are important here.)

VARIATIONS

1. Students share their ideas with the entire class. After a class discussion, each group of four writes a pamphlet showing both sides of the issue being discussed.
2. Students learn more about the topic by visiting a butcher, interviewing a vegetarian or doing research. Students add this information to their arguments.
3. Students invite a member of an animal rights group and a representative from the meat industry to visit the class. Students prepare a list of questions to ask the guests. They listen as the two guests explain and possibly argue about their points of view.

LANGUAGE CORNER: NON-VERBAL LANGUAGE

People do not communicate through language only. They also use gestures and other non-verbal behaviors such as facial expressions and "body language." Some of these gestures and non-verbal behaviors are positive and supportive. These include smiling and leaning toward the person speaking. Others show lack of cooperation. These include frowning and looking away from the speaker. It is important for students to recognize and identify behaviors that show that someone is under pressure or being uncooperative. It is also important for them to recognize and practice supportive behaviors.

Since the meaning of body language can change from one culture to another, it is important to discuss what various gestures and behaviors mean in the cultures to which students belong.

Behaviors That Demonstrate Lack of Cooperation

These include:

- frowning;
- folding the arms across the chest;
- finger pointing; and
- raising the voice.

Behaviors That Demonstrate Support

Often, non-verbal behavior can reinforce the cooperative message of the language. Some of these non-verbal behaviors vary from culture to culture. The list below provides some examples used in some cultures. Teachers might need to substitute other appropriate behaviors.

Supportive behaviors include:

- smiling;
- maintaining a relaxed posture; and
- using friendly body movement such as leaning toward the speaker.

Learn from Lectures

INTRODUCTION

Biodiversity is an important environmental concept for students to understand and appreciate. Biodiversity refers to the variety of plants and animals in a particular environment. Human actions around the world have reduced the amount of biodiversity in many areas. The listening exercise in this activity provides background on biodiversity and gives students practice both in listening for cues and note-taking.

ENVIRONMENTAL FOCUS

awareness and knowledge—understanding of biodiversity and why it is important

LANGUAGE FOCUS

listening for verbal cues, note-taking skills

LANGUAGE SKILLS

listening, writing

TIME

30 to 40 minutes

MATERIALS

Teacher Script: Biological Diversity
Blackline Master: Questions on Biodiversity
Blackline Master: Answer Key

Teacher Script: Biological Diversity

Today, I'm going to give a short lecture on biological diversity—biodiversity for short. That's spelled B-I-O-D-I-V-E-R-S-I-T-Y. During the lecture, I will explain what biodiversity is and why it is important. My lecture will have four parts. First, I will define biodiversity. Second, I will give an example of a place with a high level of biodiversity. Third, I will talk about two places with very little biodiversity. Finally, I will discuss two reasons why biodiversity is important.

Let's start with a definition of biodiversity. Biodiversity means the total variety of life. That's the total variety of life. This variety of life includes all kinds of animals and plants. The more different kinds of animals and plants there are in a place, the greater the biodiversity of that place.

Let me give you an example of a place with a great deal of biodiversity. In the Amazon jungle in South America, there is a place with a high level of biodiversity. This place is called Manu—M-A-N-U. Manu's biodiversity is higher than that of any other place on earth. In approximately three square miles (five square kilometres) in Manu, there are 550 species of birds and some 1 147 species of plants. In all of Manu, there are more than 800 species of birds, 100 species of bats and 13 species of monkeys. From this example, you can see that biodiversity simply refers to the variety in all types of life forms.

At this point, let's consider how the biodiversity level of Manu compares to the biodiversity of a golf course. What do you think? Do you think that a golf course has a high level of biodiversity? How many varieties of life do you think you can count on a golf course? Of course, there's at least one member from the mammal family: people! Then there could be three to five species of birds, several species of insects and 15 to 20 varieties of plants. It's plants that make the golf course green, right?

So where do you think you will find a golf course on the biodiversity scale? If Manu is a 100, then a golf course is what, maybe a five or six? That is, of course, not as bad as a modern concrete city, which is even lower on the scale. There is some biodiversity in a city. As long as humans are present, there are members of the mammal family. Then there are usually a lot of city animals. I'm referring to the cockroaches and rats. Cities often rate around two on a scale of biodiversity.

Now I shall move on to why biodiversity is so important. It is important for two reasons: the first is the selfish reason and the second is the ethical reason. I shall talk about the selfish reason first. This selfish reason is very much connected to the survival of us humans. You see, the greater the biodiversity of a place, the greater are the chances for scientists to discover new drugs, new foods and so on. Do you know that several species of snails do not get cancer? By studying these snails, scientists could find a cure to cancer in human beings. Do you also know that the venom—venom is poison—found in a Brazilian snake has been used to produce a drug that helps to control high blood pressure in humans? These are only two examples of how unexpected sources in nature can help humans. If we humans let the world's level of biodiversity get very low, we will have few places to look for cures for diseases such as cancer and AIDS. And that might mean that humankind itself might die off!

And now for the second reason that biodiversity is important to us: the ethical reason. The first reason was selfish. We need the plants and animals so that we can survive. The ethical reason is unselfish. The ethical reason recognizes that all forms of life—mammals, plants, insects, fish, etc.—have a right to live on this planet. We humans should not use the great power we have to kill other forms of life. Instead, we should use our power to help the plants and other animals. Remember, most of the non-human creatures on this planet are not threatening humans. It is the other way round. It is our existence, our selfish way of life, that threatens the existence of these other life forms. What gives us the right to behave as though we are the only life form that has the right to exist on planet Earth?

Answer Key:

1. d
2. c
3. (a) False
   (b) True
   (c) False
4. The biodiversity of Manu is very high. Even though the total area of Manu is very small, it has all sorts of living beings: mammals, birds, plants, insects, water creatures, etc. On the other hand, there is hardly any biodiversity on a golf course. There are only a few different plants, birds, insects and mammals.
5. It is important to conserve biodiversity because:
   (a) We need the things that can be found in places like the rainforests as resources to develop new drugs and new foods for the use of humans.
   (b) Every creature and plant has its own right to exist on this planet. They should not be made extinct just because of the careless and selfish lifestyle of humans. They have an equal right to be on earth.
6. Answers will differ. Encourage students to consider something that they or the class can do.

PREPARATION

Rehearse the short lecture by reading it aloud a few times. Alternatively, tape-record it.
Either make copies of Blackline Master: Questions on Biodiversity or place it on an overhead transparency.

PROCEDURE

1. (*Whole class*) Teach the note-taking techniques outlined in "Language Corner." It would be useful if students had already learned other note-taking techniques, such as using abbreviations or symbols, omitting redundant words and listening for cues.
2. (*Whole class*) Teacher prepares students for the lecture by telling them the title and eliciting from them what they already know about biodiversity. Teacher can explain difficult words (such as species) and write questions #4 and #5 on the board. This will prepare students to listen for specific information. Teacher instructs students to take notes while listening to the lecture and to listen for the main points instead of trying to pick up minor details such as the exact number of species of insects. This will help students to get an overall picture of what is being discussed.
3. (*Whole class*) Teacher delivers the lecture while students take notes. The lecture can be read more than once if students are having difficulty comprehending it.
4. (*Individual*) Students take three minutes to review their notes and supplement wherever necessary.
5. (*Pairs*) Students compare their notes with those of a partner.
6. (*Individual*) Teacher either distributes question sheets or displays them on the overhead. Using the notes they have taken, students answer the questions.
7. (*Pairs and Fours*) Students compare their answers with a partner and try to reach agreement. Each pair compares answers with another pair.
8. (*Whole class*) Teacher goes over answers with the students.

VARIATIONS

1. To integrate with science and mathematics, students can do surveys of the number of plant and animal species in the areas

near where they live and calculate the ratio of each species per square yard (meter) of land.

2. Students can research one aspect of biodiversity and write an essay on the topic. For example, they might learn more about the amount of biodiversity in their country, city or neighborhood.
3. Students can discuss the degree of biodiversity where they live and what can be done to promote biodiversity. They can get involved in increasing biodiversity by developing strategies for protecting wildlife habitats or growing plants that attract a variety of animal species.

LANGUAGE CORNER: LISTENING FOR VERBAL CUES

Good lecturers give cues that help listeners organize their notes. The lecture in this activity uses two types of cues. Introduce students to these types of cues so that they will take note of the information that comes immediately after the cues.

Cue #1: Use of Numbers

Using numbers tells listeners in advance how many parts there will be to the lecture or part of a lecture. This is done twice in the lecture in this activity. In the first paragraph, the lecturer explains that the lecture has four parts. The number of parts is explained again in the fifth paragraph. Note-takers can use this cue to organize their notes into sections.

Cue #2: Introducing the Main Topic

The lecturer outlines what will be said, then says it. There are many examples of this in the lecture. For instance, in the second paragraph, the lecturer says, "Let's start with a definition of biodiversity." This tells listeners that what comes next will be a definition of the term. Phrases such as "Now, I shall move on to why biodiversity is so important" tell listeners what to expect next. In this case, they will hear why biodiversity is important. Note-takers can use this type of cue to prepare for what will come next.

Questions on Biodiversity

Read the questions below. Consider the notes that you took during the lecture. Use them to decide which of the suggested answers is most correct. Place a check beside the most appropriate answer.

1. What was the lecture mainly about? The lecture was about...
   ____a. the many drugs scientists have developed from animals and plants from the tropical rainforests.
   ____b. how biodiversity can be conserved.
   ____c. the importance of places like Manu compared to the importance of places like a golf course.
   ____d. what biodiversity is and why it is important.

2. How was "biodiversity" explained in the lecture? It was explained through...
   ____a. the use of analogies, which refer to explaining something by referring to something that is similar to it but simpler to understand.
   ____b. comparing and contrasting it with other things.
   ____c. the use of examples and a comparison of the examples.
   ____d. the use of repetition.

3. Read the statements below. Place a T beside the statements that are true. Place an F beside the statements that are false.
   ____ a. Concrete cities have zero biodiversity.
   ____ b. The more kinds of animals and plants a place has, the higher its biodiversity level.
   ____ c. Animals and plants have a right to live on this planet only because they are useful to human beings.

4. Explain the general differences between the biodiversity of Manu and the biodiversity of a golf course.

____

____

____

____

5. Briefly state the reasons why it is important to conserve biodiversity.

____

____

____

____

6. What can you do to protect biodiversity where you live? What can you do to protect it elsewhere?

____

____

____

____

ADDITIONAL READING

Baines, J. & B. James. *World Resources*. New York: Simon & Schuster, 1991.

Baker, L. & A.L. Brown. "Metacognitive Skills and Reading." In *Handbook of Reading Research* (P.D. Pearson, Ed.). New York: Longman, 1984.

Barry, J., S. Siamon, & G. Huser. (Eds.). *Touch the Earth*. Toronto: Nelson Canada and The Wright Group, 1993.

Birckbichler, D.W. *Creative Activities for the Second Language Classroom*. Washington, D.C.: Center for Applied Linguistics, 1982.

Chase, J. *Blueprint for a Green School*. New York: Scholastic, 1995.

Crandall, J. (Ed.). *ESL Through Content-Area Instruction*. Englewood Cliffs, N.J.: Prentice Hall, 1987.

Dewey, J. *The School and Society*. Chicago: University of Chicago Press, 1915.

Earthworks Group. *Kid Heroes of the Environment*. Berkeley, CA: EarthWorks Group, 1991.

EarthWorks Group. *The Student Environmental Action Guide*. Berkeley, CA: EarthWorks Group, 1991.

Fountain, S. *Education for Development: A Teacher's Resource for Global Learning*. London: Heinemann Educational Books, 1995.

Freire, P. *Pedagogy of the Oppressed*. New York: Seabury Press, 1968.

Ghafoor-Ghaznawi, A. "Environmental Education: Recent Trends and Perspectives." Paper presented at the Seminar on Education for Environmental Competence, Singapore, February, 1993.

Grant, J.E. *The Kids' Green Plan: How to Write Your Own Plan to Save the Environment*. Bothell, WA: The Wright Group, 1993.

Greenpeace Canada. *The Carbon Bomb*. Toronto: Greenpeace Canada, 1995.

Greig, S., G. Pike, & D. Selby. *Earthrights: Education As If the Planet Really Mattered*. London: Kogan Page, 1987.

Guilford, J.P. *Intelligence, Creativity, and their Educational Implications*. New York: Robert R. Knapp, 1968.

Holt, D.D. *Cooperative Learning: A Response to Linguistic and Cultural Diversity*. Washington, D.C.: Center for Applied Linguistics, 1993.

Howe, R.W. & J.F. Disinger. *Environmental Activities for Teaching Critical Thinking*. ERIC Clearinghouse for Science, Mathematics, and Environmental Education, 1990.

Jacobs, G.M. *Integrating Environmental Education in Second Language Instruction*. Singapore: SEAMEO Regional Language Center, 1993.

Jacobs, G.M. "Developing Materials with an Environmental Focus." In *Getting Started: Materials Writers on Materials Writing* (A.C. Hidalgo, D. Hall, & G.M Jacobs, Eds.). Singapore: SEAMEO Regional Language Center, 1995.

Kagan, S. *Cooperative Learning*. San Clemente, CA: Kagan Cooperative Learning, 1992.

Lim, K. *The Green Age Textbook*. Singapore: Federal Publications, 1992.

Mason, A. *The Green Classroom*. Bothell, WA: The Wright Group, 1993.

McCallum, R. & R. Whitlow. *Linking Mathematics and Language*. Toronto: Pippin Publishing, 1994.

Munby, H. "Metaphor in the Thinking of Teachers: An Exploratory Study." In *Journal of Curriculum Studies*. Vol. 18, (1986).

Rivers, W. *Speaking in Many Tongues: Essays in Foreign Language Teaching*. (2nd ed.). Rowley, MA: Newbury House, 1976.

Stempleski, S. *Focus on the Environment*. Englewood Cliffs, N.J.: Prentice Hall, 1992.

Stempleski, S. *Earthwatch*. Englewood Cliffs, N.J.: Prentice Hall, 1992.

Slavin, R.E. *Cooperative Learning: Theory, Research, and Practice*. Englewood Cliffs, N.J.: Prentice Hall, 1990.

Thornbury, S. "Metaphors We Work By: EFL and Its Metaphors." In *ELT Journal*. Vol. 45 (1991).

Uppal, D.K. *Students as Environment Communicators: An Alternative Model*. Sagar, India: Department of Mass Communication and Journalism, University of Sagar, 1988.

Utami Munandar, S.C. and C. Semiawan. *Approaches to Enhance Children's Creativity in Indonesia*. Clearinghouse for Information on Women in Development and the Creativity Development Foundation, 1988.

Wenden, A. *Learner Strategies for Learner Autonomy*. Englewood Cliffs, N.J.: Prentice Hall, 1991.

World Resources Institute. *Energy, Atmosphere and Climate*. Washington, D.C.: World Resources Institute, 1994.

USEFUL MAGAZINES

E Magazine, PO Box 2047, Marion, OH 43305 USA

The Green Teacher, 95 Robert Street, Toronto, ON M5S 2K5 CANADA

Resurgence Magazine, Rocksea Farmhouse, St. Mabyn Bodmin, Cornwall PL30 3BR UNITED KINGDOM

USEFUL WEBSITES

The Green Teacher—http://www.web.ca/~greentea/

Resurgence Magazine—http://www.gn.apc.org/resurgence/

United Nations Environment Programme—
http://www.unchs.unon.org/

World Wildlife Fund (also known as WWF or World Wide Fund for Nature)—http://www.panda.org/